**Scan the QR Code below
for more information
on Terry's work:**

To:

_____

From:

_____

Date:

_____

Quotation Sources by Permission:

AMP Amplified Bible © 1954, 1958, 1962, 1964, 1965, 1987. Lockman Foundation.

CEV Contemporary English Version © 1991, 1992, 1995. American Bible Society.

ESV The Holy Bible, English Standard Version © 2001. Crossway, a publishing ministry of Good News Publishers.

ISV International Standard Version © 1996-2008. ISV Foundation.

KJV King James Version.

MEV The Holy Bible, Modern English Version © 2014. Charisma House.

MSG The Message © 1993. NavPress Publishing Group.

NABRE New American Bible Revised Edition © 2011. Confraternity of Christian Doctrine.

NASB New American Standard Bible © 1960, 1962, 1963, 1968, 1971, 1972, 1973, 1975, 1977, 1988, 1995. Lockman Foundation.

NET New English Translation Bible © 1996-2003. Biblical Studies Press.

NIV The Holy Bible, New International Version © 1973, 1978, 1984. International Bible Society.

NLT The New Living Translation © 1996, 2004, 2007, 2013, 2015. Tyndale House Foundation. Tyndale House Publishers.

TLB The Living Bible © 1971. Tyndale House Publishers.

TPT The Passion Translation © 2017, 2018. Passion & Fire Ministries.

VOICE The Voice © 2012. Thomas Nelson.

All songs, lyrics, and poetry are public domain.

Cover and interior design by Kathryn Krogh
Author photo by Kimberly Krauk

ISBN: 9781734112221

Lively Hope
BOOKS & MORE

RADIANCE OF *Jesus*

ONE HUNDRED DEVOTIONS

*The Son is the radiance of God's glory and
the exact representation of his being,
sustaining all things by his powerful word.*

HEBREWS 1:3A

TERRY WARD
TUCKER

YOUR JOURNEY IN DIVINE LIGHT

Walk in the Radiance of Jesus,
God's own Glory. He will light your path.
For Jesus is God's flow'r, whose fragrance,
tender with sweetness, fills the air, and dispels
with glorious splendor the darkness everywhere.
"LO, HOW A ROSE E'ER BLOOMING" FRIEDRICH LAYRITZ

Thank you, Heavenly Father, for C. S. Lewis'
inspired certainty that Jesus is, indeed, your Son,
my Savior, and Light of the World. Lewis wrote:
"I believe in Christianity as I believe that the sun has
risen, not only because I see it, but because by it I see
everything else." In the Light of Jesus' name,
I am grateful he, too, has risen. Amen.

The Son is the radiance of God's glory
and exact representation of his being.
HEBREWS 1:3A NIV

✦—————— HEART THOUGHTS ——————✦

Jesus blesses me with his Light when he ....

....

....

....

....

....

....

....

....

....

✦—————— PRAYER OF GRATITUDE ——————✦

Today, I'm thankful for ....

....

....

....

....

....

....

....

....

....

Date _____

DEFINITION OF DIVINE LIGHT

God's Light in Jesus is purity, goodness,
perfection, righteousness, sovereignty, life,
love, truth, glory, radiance, absence of darkness,
absence of evil, sinlessness, salvation, gospel,
justice, worthy of worship/praise/honor/
gratitude/submission/obedience,
kindness, forgiveness, mercy, grace, faithfulness,
omnipotence, omniscience, eternity, mystery,
transcendence, immanence, Creator, Father, Jesus,
Spirit, wisdom, generosity, patience, knowledge,
supernatural, Savior, holy, and more.
How deep is the meaning in God's Light!

God is light, pure light;
there's not a trace of darkness in him.
1 JOHN 1:5B MSG

Thank you, Father, in Jesus' name that he is my
saving Radiance. He is all things good. Amen.

His cloud-brightness is like dawn, exploding,
spreading, forked-lightning shooting from his hand -
what power is hidden in that fist!
HABAKKUK 3:3B-4 MSG

HEART THOUGHTS

Jesus blesses me with his Light when he ....

....

....

....

....

....

....

....

....

....

PRAYER OF GRATITUDE

Today, I'm thankful for ....

....

....

....

....

....

....

....

....

....

Date _____

UNDERSTANDING JESUS' LIGHT

Your Heavenly Father loves you so much that he opened your mind to the concept of his Holy Light. He even taught you to associate his Light with Jesus' pure righteousness. God knows you cannot understand him totally, but he chose to give you enough knowledge of his Light of Righteousness to make you grateful for your salvation in the Radiance of his Son.

God is Light,
and in Him there is no darkness at all.
1 JOHN 1:5B NASB

Father, thank you in Jesus' name that he sums up your Holy Light of Righteousness, Life, and Love. I am grateful my Savior covered me in salvation with his own perfection. Amen.

He (God) made Him (Jesus) who knew no sin to
be sin on our behalf, so that we might become
the Righteousness of God in Him.
2 CORINTHIANS 5:21 NASB

DAY ③

Jesus blesses me with his Light when he ....

....

....

....

....

....

....

....

....

....

✦ ———— PRAYER OF GRATITUDE ———— ✦

Today, I'm thankful for ....

....

....

....

....

....

....

....

....

....

Date _____

CLEANSING POWER
OF JESUS' LIGHT

God forgave your sins and washed you clean
in the blood of Jesus. Then he anointed
you with his own Light of Righteousness.
You are clean in your Savior.

God is God, he has bathed us in light. Festoon the
shrine with garlands, hang colored banners above the
altar! Thank God — he's so good. His love never quits!
PSALM 118:27; 29 MSG

In your name, Jesus, thank you for shining
away my sins with your purity and saving
me by your grace of forgiving love. Amen.

The light of God's love shone within us
when he sent his matchless Son into the
world so that we might live through him.
1 JOHN 4:9 TPT

❖—————— HEART THOUGHTS ——————❖

Jesus blesses me with his Light when he ....

....

....

....

....

....

....

....

....

....

❖—————— PRAYER OF GRATITUDE ——————❖

Today, I'm thankful for ....

....

....

....

....

....

....

....

....

....

Date _____

GOD'S LIGHT OF LOVE - JESUS!

To understand how God manifests salvation's
love and light in your heart by the power
of the Holy Spirit, consider Jesus' trustworthy
declaration that he is Light of the World.
Yes, the Savior is God's sacred
illumination of his love for you.

*The Light of God's love shone within us when he
sent his matchless Son into the world so that we might
live through him. This is love: He loved us long before
we loved him. It was his love, not ours. He proved it
by sending his Son to be the pleasing sacrificial
offering to take away our sins.*

1 JOHN 4:9-10 TPT

Thank you, Father, in Jesus' name
for his gift of Life-Light that is your
unselfish Love for me. Amen.

*Delightfully loved ones, if he (Jesus) loved
us with such tremendous love,
then loving one another should be our way of life!*

1 JOHN 4:11 TPT

DAY (5)

Jesus blesses me with his Light when he ....

....

....

....

....

....

....

....

....

....

✦ ———————— PRAYER OF GRATITUDE ———————— ✦

Today, I'm thankful for ....

....

....

....

....

....

....

....

....

....

Date _____

JESUS, THE SON - GOD'S OWN GLORY

God's Glory Light is too bright for human eyes to behold, but he loved you so much that he caused his Light to be accessible to you in his Son, for Jesus himself is the righteous brilliance of God's Glory.

And the Word (Jesus) was made flesh, and dwelt among us, and we beheld his glory, the glory as of the only begotten Son of the Father, full of grace and truth.
JOHN 1:14 KJV

Father God, thank you in the bright name of
Jesus for enveloping me in Salvation Radiance.
Your Holy Spirit now lives in my heart,
making Christ's Light my Light.
I glorify you in your divine Light -
Father, Son, and Holy Spirit.
Glory! Glory! Glory! Amen.

[Simeon] He (Jesus) is a light to reveal God to the nations, and he is the glory of your people Israel!"
LUKE 2:32 NLT

✦ ——————— HEART THOUGHTS ——————— ✦

Jesus blesses me with his Light when he ....

....

....

....

....

....

....

....

....

....

✦ ——————— PRAYER OF GRATITUDE ——————— ✦

Today, I'm thankful for ....

....

....

....

....

....

....

....

....

....

Date _____

FINDING YOUR WAY
BY GOD'S LIGHT

Just as God's *sun*light dispels natural darkness
enabling you to see where you are walking
physically, his divine *Son*Light - JESUS! -
dispels malevolent darkness enabling you to
see where you are walking Spiritually.

*This, in essence, is the message we heard from Christ
and are passing on to you: God is light, pure light;
there's not a trace of darkness in him.*
1 JOHN 1:5 MSG

Thank you, Father, for *sun*light that gives me
physical awareness of the natural world.
But thank you more for Jesus' *Son*Light that
gives me divine awareness of the Spiritual
world, for Jesus is your authentic Savior,
authentic Word, and authentic Light.
I pray in his celestial name. Amen.

*By your words I can see where I'm going;
they throw a beam of light on my dark path.*
PSALM 119:105 MSG

DAY (7)

Jesus blesses me with his Light when he ....

....

....

....

....

....

....

....

....

....

PRAYER OF GRATITUDE

Today, I'm thankful for ....

....

....

....

....

....

....

....

....

....

Date _____

DARKNESS OF EVIL CONQUERED

When you accepted Jesus as God's Son and your Savior, he gave you his own eternal Light of Life.

The Word was first, the Word present to God,
God present to the Word. The Word was God,
in readiness for God from day one. Everything was
created through him; nothing – not one thing! –
came into being without him. What came into
existence was Life, and Life was Light to live by.
The Life-Light blazed out of the darkness;
the darkness could not put it out.

JOHN 1:1-5 MSG

In Jesus' name - God's Son and Radiant Word -
I pray to be a living torch of his Light that
through me he may heal others by the same
forgiving grace with which he healed me.
Amen.

Sweetly the Light has dawned upon me;
Once I was blind, but now I can see:
The Light of the world is Jesus!

PHILIP PAUL BLISS

DAY (8)

Jesus blesses me with his Light when he ....

....

....

....

....

....

....

....

....

....

—————— PRAYER OF GRATITUDE ——————

Today, I'm thankful for ....

....

....

....

....

....

....

....

....

....

Date _____

DAY 9

JESUS' LIGHT OF SALVATION

Testify, good John the Baptist! Witness that
Jesus is God's Life Light. Preach confession
and remission of sin. Preach baptism.
Preach salvation in our Heavenly Father's Son.
Preach His Holy Radiance and Divinity.
Testify, good John the Baptist!

*A man came, one sent from God, and his name
was John (John the Baptist). He came as a witness
to testify about the Light (Jesus), so that all might
believe through him. He (John) was not the Light,
but he came to testify about the Light.*

JOHN 1:6-8 NASB

Thank you, God, for John the Baptist.
He preached Jesus who forgave and saved me
by grace and covered me in his own purity,
which made me acceptable to pray directly
to you. In my Savior's merciful name, Amen.

*This (Jesus) was the true Light that, coming into
the world, enlightens every person. And as many
as received Him, to them He gave the right to become
children of God, to those who believed in His name.*

JOHN 1:9; 12 NASB

DAY (9)

Jesus blesses me with his Light when he ....

....

....

....

....

....

....

....

....

....

⟶ ———— PRAYER OF GRATITUDE ———— ⟵

Today, I'm thankful for ....

....

....

....

....

....

....

....

....

....

Date _____

CERTAIN HOPE IN JESUS' LIGHT

Ask God to help you see everything in your life by the Light of Jesus' Love. Keep your Spiritual eyes trained on him as through faith you receive the power of his blessed hope.

[Paul] I pray the eyes of your heart may be enlightened in order that you may know the hope to which he has called you, the riches of his glorious inheritance in his holy people, and his incomparably great power for us who believe.
EPHESIANS 1:18-19A NIV

Awesome God, I am grateful every morning when I see dawn's fresh beauty shining hope on a new day, which gives me remembrance of Jesus, your Holy Dawn. He is my Savior in whose transcendent name I pray all gratitude for the confidence he shines into my heart. Thank you, Father, for life eternal in your Kingdom and for your Son's Light of Assured Hope. Amen.

[David] Suddenly, GOD, you floodlight my life; I'm blazing with glory, God's glory!
PSALM 18:28 MSG

DAY (10)

Jesus blesses me with his Light when he ....

....

....

....

....

....

....

....

....

....

✦——————— PRAYER OF GRATITUDE ——————✦

Today, I'm thankful for ....

....

....

....

....

....

....

....

....

....

Date _____

COUNTENANCE OF GOD
IN JESUS' LIGHT

Jesus, the Son, is the eternal Light of your
Heavenly Father's expression of Love.

Lift up the Light of your countenance upon us,
O LORD! You have put gladness in my heart.
PSALM 4:6B-7A NASB 1995

Thank you, God, for your comforting
expression that shines forth from Jesus' face.
He is the only Life-Light I will ever need.
Let me bask in his Joy-Light as I commune
with the Spirit in the Son's Joy-Radiance.
Teach me, Father, to shine my Savior's peace
on others. I pray in his name. Amen.

(Aaron, brother of Moses) The Lord bless you and
keep you; the Lord make his face to shine upon
you and be gracious to you; the Lord lift up his
countenance upon you and give you peace.
NUMBERS 6:24-26 ESV

HEART THOUGHTS

Jesus blesses me with his Light when he ....

....

....

....

....

....

....

....

....

....

PRAYER OF GRATITUDE

Today, I'm thankful for ....

....

....

....

....

....

....

....

....

....

Date _____

GOD'S LIGHT OF LEARNING

Seek God's path to Spiritual instruction through
his words of Truth and Light. Then take Jesus'
hand as he extends it to help you obey.

*The unfolding of your words (God's words)
gives Light; It gives understanding to the simple.
Make your face shine upon your servant
and teach me your decrees.*
PSALM 119:130; 135 NIV

Thank you, God, that when I seek your
Spiritual enlightenment, I find it in Jesus.
He is the Word and the Light out of whose
mouth issues Truth brighter in clarity than
sunlit air and sharper in accuracy than a
two-edged sword. I pray in his name -
God's Word, Light of the World. Amen.

*God means what he says. What he says goes.
His powerful Word is as sharp as a surgeon's scalpel,
cutting through everything, whether doubt or defense,
laying us open to listen and obey.*
HEBREWS 4:12 MSG

DAY (12)

Jesus blesses me with his Light when he ....

....

....

....

....

....

....

....

....

....

━━━━━ PRAYER OF GRATITUDE ━━━━━

Today, I'm thankful for ....

....

....

....

....

....

....

....

....

....

Date _____

Jesus' Radiance –
Your Light to God's Pathway

Attention, believers! Follow Christ's road of uprightness, for his Light dispels evil's darkness and his face shines with salvation.

The way of the righteous is like the first gleam of dawn, which shines ever brighter until the full light of day. But the way of the wicked is like total darkness. They have no idea what they are stumbling over.

Proverbs 4:18-19 NLT

Thank you, Jesus, for guiding me along life's path. By your Light, my way is clear. In your presence, my heart is confident. Glorify you, shining Savior. Accept my gratitude as I pray in your awesome name. You make my life's journey glow with gladness. Amen.

You pulled me from the brink of death, my feet from the cliff-edge of doom. Now I stroll at leisure with God in the sunlit fields of life.

Psalm 56:13 MSG

✦ —————— HEART THOUGHTS —————— ✦

Jesus blesses me with his Light when he ....

....

....

....

....

....

....

....

....

....

✦ —————— PRAYER OF GRATITUDE —————— ✦

Today, I'm thankful for ....

....

....

....

....

....

....

....

....

....

Date _____

DAY 14

Jesus' Light in You

Ask your Savior to give you grace to share
his Holy Radiance with others as he
shares so generously with you.

*Men and women who have lived wisely and well
will shine brilliantly, like the cloudless,
star-strewn night skies. And those who put others on
the right path to life will glow like stars forever.*
Daniel 12:3 MSG

Father, just as dark areas on a painting make
light areas appear brighter by contrast, let the
enemy's evil accusations against me cause my life
to shine brighter with my Savior's forgiving Light,
for Jesus is the preeminent contrast to evil's
darkness. I pray in his luminous name. Amen.

*[Jesus] Here's another way to put it: You're here to
be light, bringing out the God-colors in the world.
God is not a secret to be kept. We're going public
with this, as public as a city on a hill.*
Matthew 5:14 MSG

✦———— HEART THOUGHTS ————✦

Jesus blesses me with his Light when he ....

....

....

....

....

....

....

....

....

....

✦———— PRAYER OF GRATITUDE ————✦

Today, I'm thankful for ....

....

....

....

....

....

....

....

....

....

Date _____

JESUS' REFRACTED LIGHT - HOLY SON, WHOLLY DEITY!

Your Heavenly Father's arc in the sky is his pledge of promise - *no more world-destroying floods.* How merciful is our God!

From now on, when I form a cloud over the Earth and the rainbow forms in the cloud, I'll remember my covenant between me and you and everything living, that never again will floodwaters destroy all life.

GENESIS 9:14-15 MSG

In your name, thank you, Jesus, for natural sunlight with its hidden colors, the full spectrum of which can be seen only through a prism. What a lovely metaphor for the multitude of sacred secrets within your divine Light. Your creations are exquisite, Savior, as are you. Amen.

[Ezekiel's vision of Jesus) From the waist up he looked like burnished bronze and from the waist down like a blazing fire. Brightness everywhere! The way a rainbow springs out of the sky on a rainy day. It turned out to be the Glory of God!

EZEKIEL 1:27-28 MSG

— HEART THOUGHTS —

Jesus blesses me with his Light when he ....

....

....

....

....

....

....

....

....

....

— PRAYER OF GRATITUDE —

Today, I'm thankful for ....

....

....

....

....

....

....

....

....

Date _____

YOU - Born to Glorify Your Heavenly Father in His Son

Jesus, your Heavenly Father's own Light filled
you with his Radiance in the Spirit at your
salvation. Glorify him in the Holy Trinity
by sharing his *Son*Light with others.
You exist to exalt God!

Let your light so shine before men in such a
way that they may see your good works
and glorify your Father who is in heaven.

Matthew 5:16 mev

Father, I glorify you with all my heart.
You rescued me from sin and death by the power
of your Son's pure blood. He is your Light, Life,
and Love all shared with me, your saved child.
Be glorified in His Name, Light of the World.
Glory, Glory, Glory! Jesus, Jesus, Jesus! Amen.

And my God will meet all your needs according to
the richness of his glory in Christ Jesus. To our
God and Father be glory forever and ever. Amen.

Philippians 4:19-20 niv

✦ ——— HEART THOUGHTS ——— ✦

Jesus blesses me with his Light when he ....

....

....

....

....

....

....

....

....

....

✦ ——— PRAYER OF GRATITUDE ——— ✦

Today, I'm thankful for ....

....

....

....

....

....

....

....

....

....

Date _____

Faith in the Light of Jesus

Though clouds sometimes block the sun,
you know by faith it still shines. And though
clouds of life sometimes block Jesus' Light,
you know by faith He, too, still shines.

[God] But for you who revere my name, the sun of
righteousness will rise with healing in its rays.

Malachi 2:4a niv

Thank you, God, that your prophet,
Malachi, used the phrase, sun of righteousness,
to point toward Jesus, your only begotten
Son of Righteousness. Malachi comforted us by
declaring Jesus would rise and heal our
hearts with salvation hidden in his Light.
We rejoice in Jesus' divine Radiance.
In his saving name, Son of Righteousness,
we pray our thanks. Glorify Him in the Godhead -
Father, Son, and Holy Spirit! Amen.

Wake up sleeper, rise from the dead,
and Christ will shine on you.

Ephesians 5:14b niv

✦ ———— HEART THOUGHTS ———— ✦

Jesus blesses me with his Light when he ....

....

....

....

....

....

....

....

....

....

✦ ———— PRAYER OF GRATITUDE ———— ✦

Today, I'm thankful for ....

....

....

....

....

....

....

....

....

....

Date _____

REFRESHMENT IN JESUS' LIGHT

Jesus' Holy Radiance can be subtle or bright depending on your need. You never have to worry whether his Spiritual wattage will fit your situation. His eternal uncreated Light will guard and restore you in every circumstance.

*[Jesus] I am the Root and Branch of David,
the Bright Morning Star.*
REVELATION 22:16B MSG

Thank you, God, for Jesus – your subtle dawn, radiant sunrise, dazzling daylight, bright daystar, purple twilight, twinkling starlight, mysterious moonlight, all in unity with your own Holy Light. In the Son's name, thank you, Father God, that He is one with you, one with the Spirit, and one with believers, yet complete in Himself and worthy to shine His Glory Light on all creation. Amen.

*We couldn't be more sure of what we saw and heard –
God's glory, God's voice. The prophetic Word (Jesus)
was confirmed to us. He's the one light you have
in a dark time as you wait for daybreak and the
rising Morning Star in your hearts.*
2 PETER 1:19 MSG

✦ ——— HEART THOUGHTS ——— ✦

Jesus blesses me with his Light when he ....

....

....

....

....

....

....

....

....

....

✦ ——— PRAYER OF GRATITUDE ——— ✦

Today, I'm thankful for ....

....

....

....

....

....

....

....

....

....

Date _____

Bright Morning of Jesus' Radiance

Natural starlight against the backdrop of
a night sky is a beautiful metaphor for the
divine Light of Jesus, God's victor over
sin's gloom and death's hopelessness.
Be gone, dark night! Welcome, bright morning!
Welcome, Savior!

*O holy night, the stars are brightly shining. It is the
night of the dear Savior's birth. Long lay the world in
sin and error pining, 'til he appeared, and the soul
felt its worth. A thrill of hope the weary world rejoices,
for yonder breaks a new and glorious morn!*

PLACIDE CAPPEAU

In your name, thank you, Jesus, for coming to
earth to banish all shadow of sin. Even stars
lose their brilliance alongside the Father's
Heavenly Light that he ushered in at your birth.
I pray my gratitude for his Holy Radiance.
Amen.

*For those who live in a dark land,
the Light (Jesus) will shine on them.*

ISAIAH 9:2B NASB

HEART THOUGHTS

Jesus blesses me with his Light when he ....

....

....

....

....

....

....

....

....

....

PRAYER OF GRATITUDE

Today, I'm thankful for ....

....

....

....

....

....

....

....

....

....

Date _____

Your Life in Jesus' Light

God quickens and sustains physical life.
You consume plants that use created sunlight in
photosynthesis to make sugars to support energy
and growth - miraculous! Yet, more miraculous,
God quickens and sustains Spiritual life as the
Holy Spirit fills and fuels you at your salvation
with the energy of Jesus' Holy Radiance.

In him (Jesus) was Life,
and that Life was the Light of all mankind.
John 1:4 NIV

Thank you, God, in Jesus' name that the created
life you gave to plants, animals, and humans was
not the first life. You in your Holy Trinity are the
uncreated Life Light that always was and always
will be. I pray my gratitude for your loving
gift of eternal Life Light. Amen.

For you (God) are the fountain of Life,
the Light by which we see.
Psalm 36:9 NLT

HEART THOUGHTS

Jesus blesses me with his Light when he ....

....

....

....

....

....

....

....

....

....

PRAYER OF GRATITUDE

Today, I'm thankful for ....

....

....

....

....

....

....

....

....

....

Date _____

DAY 21

Vast Power of Jesus' Light

Joseph's father, Jacob, gave him a coat of many colors because he loved him, just as God gave you Jesus, his own divine Light because he loved you. Let the bright colors in Joseph's coat point you toward Jesus' sacred Light that if refracted would reveal the myriad of holy attributes within his character. For Jesus' Light is divine, uncreated, and multidimensional in its power.

Now Israel (Jacob) loved Joseph more than all his children, for he was the son of his old age: And he made him a coat of many colours.
Genesis 37:3 kjv

Father, in Jesus' name, thank you for loving me enough to cloak me in your Son's protective covering that is his own shining coat - His Light of Salvation Life. Amen.

Believe in the Light (Jesus) while you have the Light, so that you may become children of Light.
John 12:36b niv

→ ——— HEART THOUGHTS ——— ←

Jesus blesses me with his Light when he ....

....

....

....

....

....

....

....

....

....

→ ——— PRAYER OF GRATITUDE ——— ←

Today, I'm thankful for ....

....

....

....

....

....

....

....

....

....

Date _____

DAY 22

GOOD FRUIT - THAT WHICH FLOURISHES IN THE SPIRIT'S LIGHT

Do you want to languish in Satan's darkness where you will shrivel unto death bearing no good fruit, or blossom in Jesus' Light where you will thrive bearing God's pure fruit of the Spirit?

God-Light streamed into the world (from Jesus), but men and women everywhere ran for darkness. They went for darkness, because they were not really interested in pleasing God. But anyone living in truth and reality welcomes God-light, so the work can be seen for the God-work that it is.

JOHN 3:19B; 21 MSG

Jesus, I choose God-Light in you over darkness in Satan. In your name, Savior, I pray to honor you by working within your transparent Life-Light to produce virtuous fruit of the Spirit. Glorify You, Father! Glorify You, Son! Glorify You, Holy Spirit! Amen.

But the fruit of the Spirit is love, joy, peace, patience, kindness, goodness, faithfulness, gentleness, and self-control.

GALATIANS 5:22-23A ESV

✦———— HEART THOUGHTS ————✦

Jesus blesses me with his Light when he ....

....

....

....

....

....

....

....

....

....

✦———— PRAYER OF GRATITUDE ————✦

Today, I'm thankful for ....

....

....

....

....

....

....

....

....

....

Date _____

CLEAR VISION IN JESUS' LIGHT

What good will it do in the eternal to have twenty/twenty vision in your Heavenly Father's physical light if you remain blind - *on purpose* - to Jesus' Spiritual Light?

Open my eyes to see the wonderful truths in God's instructions.
PSALM 119:18 NLT

Thank you, Father, in Jesus' name for enabling me to see physically when natural light hits my retinas, the process of which turns the rays into electrical impulses that my brain interprets as images. But thank you more for saving me to see Spiritually by the Light of Jesus, who, on entering my heart by the power of the Spirit, interprets the Light of God as His Word and Truth. I choose the Father, Jesus, and the Spirit - all three God's Light! Amen.

[Jesus to Paul] I'm sending you off to open the eyes of outsiders so they can see the difference between dark and light, see the difference between Satan and God, and choose God.
ACTS 26:17-18A MSG

DAY 23

──────── HEART THOUGHTS ────────

Jesus blesses me with his Light when he ....

....

....

....

....

....

....

....

....

....

──────── PRAYER OF GRATITUDE ────────

Today, I'm thankful for ....

....

....

....

....

....

....

....

....

....

....

Date _____

JESUS' RADIANCE - GOD'S ENLIGHTENMENT FOR YOU!

Find help with life's challenges by asking God to lead you through Scripture to his Son's Light of Understanding. For Jesus is your Savior, God's Word, Son in the Trinity, and wholly God himself. Praise him for enlightening you by the Spirit's teaching in the Word.

Thy word is a lamp unto my feet,
and a light unto my path.

PSALM 119:105 KJV

Father, thank you in Jesus' name that his Light of Learning is available to me in Scripture, the meaning of which your Holy Spirit reveals whenever I pray for understanding. Your Spirit shows me Spiritual Truths by the Radiance of Jesus, your Son and Word. In his name, I pray my gratitude for divine guidance and wisdom. Let me shine his Truth on others! Amen.

[Jesus] It is the Spirit who gives life;
the flesh is no help at all. The words that
I have spoken to you are spirit and life.

JOHN 6:63 ESV

HEART THOUGHTS

Jesus blesses me with his Light when he ....

....

....

....

....

....

....

....

....

....

PRAYER OF GRATITUDE

Today, I'm thankful for ....

....

....

....

....

....

....

....

....

....

Date _____

STAR OF BETHLEHEM -
SHINING SIGNAL OF JESUS' LIGHT

Christmas star, calm and bright, beam of hope
in dark night, gift to the world, salvation's pearl,
Son of God – JESUS!

*Silent night, holy night, All is calm, all is bright.
'Round yon virgin Mother and child. Holy infant
so tender and mild. Sleep in heavenly peace.
Sleep in heavenly peace.*

FRANZ GRUBER AND JOSEPH MOHR

Thank you, God, for your special Star of Light
that in silence of darkness guided the wise
men to newborn Jesus. They sought and found
him by the brilliant star you provided to
illumine their way. In the Savior's name, I pray
my gratitude for your singular star. Amen.

*And, lo, the star, which they saw in the east,
went before them, till it came and stood over where the
young child was. When they saw the star, they rejoiced
with exceeding great joy. And when they were come
into the house, they saw the young child with Mary
his mother, and fell down and worshipped him.*

MATTHEW 2:9B-11A KJV

HEART THOUGHTS

Jesus blesses me with his Light when he ....

....

....

....

....

....

....

....

....

....

PRAYER OF GRATITUDE

Today, I'm thankful for ....

....

....

....

....

....

....

....

....

....

Date _____

Aglow with Jesus' Radiance

Which kind of mirror is your life – a living
mirror reflecting Jesus' vibrant countenance or
a dead mirror reflecting self's dull lifelessness?

But we as Christians have no veils over our faces;
we can be mirrors that brightly reflect the glory of
the Lord (Jesus). And as the Spirit of Jesus works
within us, we become more and more like him.

2 Corinthians 3:18 tlb

For if any be a hearer of the word, and not a doer, he
is like unto a man beholding his natural face in a glass:
For he beholdeth himself, and goeth his way, and
straightway forgetteth what manner of man he was.

James 1:23-24 kjv

In your name, Jesus, I pray to reflect God's loving
Radiance that is also You, Righteous Son. Amen.

[Jesus] Whoever looks at me is looking, in fact,
at the One (God) who sent me. I am Light that
has come into the world, so that all who believe
in me won't have to stay any longer in the dark.

John 12:46b msg

✦——— HEART THOUGHTS ———✦

Jesus blesses me with his Light when he ....

....

....

....

....

....

....

....

....

....

✦——— PRAYER OF GRATITUDE ———✦

Today, I'm thankful for ....

....

....

....

....

....

....

....

....

....

Date _____

DAY 27

NEW VITALITY IN JESUS' RADIANCE

Human beings suffer miserably from deprivation
of physical light. And yet how much more we
suffer from deprivation of Jesus' Spiritual Light.
Be grateful for Isaiah's prophecy that our
Savior's Light will heal those who believe in him.

[Isaiah about Jesus and his saved ones]
Then your Light will break forth like the dawn,
and your healing will quickly appear;
then your righteousness will go before you,
and the glory of the Lord will be your rear guard.
ISAIAH 58:8 NIV

Thank you, God, for saving me in your Son.
His Light of Righteousness regenerated
me into a new creature by the power of the
Holy Spirit, restoring my sin-sick soul through
his grace of forgiveness and salvation.
In my Savior's name, accept my gratitude. Amen.

Let all that I am praise the LORD; may I never
forget the good things he does for me.
He forgives all my sins and heals all my diseases.
PSALM 103:2-3 NLT

✦——————— **HEART THOUGHTS** ———————✦

Jesus blesses me with his Light when he ....

....

....

....

....

....

....

....

....

....

✦——————— **PRAYER OF GRATITUDE** ———————✦

Today, I'm thankful for ....

....

....

....

....

....

....

....

....

....

Date _____

LIGHT SOURCE OF HEAVEN - GOD'S OWN GLORY

In which direction are you marching –
toward God's City of Light called Zion or
Satan's region of darkness called hell?

We're marching to Zion, beautiful, beautiful Zion.
We're marching upward to Zion, beautiful city of God.
ISAAC WATTS

From the dazzle of Zion, God blazes into view
(prophecy of Messiah Jesus). Our God makes
his entrance. He's not shy in coming.
Starbursts of fireworks precede him.
PSALM 50:2-3 MSG

Thank you, Father, for John the Revelator's
prophetic description of Zion, New Jerusalem.
Glorify the Lamb-Lamp of Zion - King Jesus!

[John] For the temple (in New Jerusalem) is the Lord
God Almighty and the Lamb (Jesus). And the city has
no need of sun or moon to shine on it, for the glory of
God gives it light and its lamp is the Lamb.
REVELATION 21:22B-23 ESV

✦ ——— HEART THOUGHTS ——— ✦

Jesus blesses me with his Light when he ....

....

....

....

....

....

....

....

....

....

✦ ——— PRAYER OF GRATITUDE ——— ✦

Today, I'm thankful for ....

....

....

....

....

....

....

....

....

....

Date _____

NATURAL SKY LIGHTS - REMINDERS OF GOD'S GLORY

Your Heavenly Father shows you suggestions of
his own Glory Light in the extravagant beauty of
physical light. Gaze at the sky day or night to
experience God's awesome gifts of
created light…from stunning sunrises and
sunsets to subtle moonlight and starlight,
all of which pale next to Jesus, the Son,
our Father's Brilliant Glory Light.

Be exalted, God, above the heavens.
May your glory shine throughout the earth.
PSALM 57:11 TLB

Thank you, Jesus, in your name for using
sky lights to remind me of your Holy Radiance.
Fair is the sunshine, Fairer still the moonlight, and all
the twinkling, starry host. Jesus shines brighter.
Jesus shines purer than all the angels heav'n can boast.
JOHN SEISS

There was the true Light (Jesus) which,
coming into the world, enlightens every man.
JOHN 1:9 NASB 1995

DAY 29

─── HEART THOUGHTS ───

Jesus blesses me with his Light when he ....

....

....

....

....

....

....

....

....

....

─── PRAYER OF GRATITUDE ───

Today, I'm thankful for ....

....

....

....

....

....

....

....

....

....

Date _____

JESUS - LIGHT OF THE WORLD AND YOU - LIGHT OF THE WORLD

Your salvation in Jesus is transforming you from one degree to another into the glory of his image, for he has given you his Light to share with others. He wants you to shine as he shines – Light of the World!

And we all, with unveiled faces, beholding the glory of the Lord, are being transformed into the same image from one degree of glory to another. For this comes from the Lord who is the Spirit.

2 CORINTHIANS 3:18 ESV

In Jesus' name, thank you, Father, that your Son is perfecting me in his own Light-filled image in preparation for his return. Let me glow brighter day by day in his Radiance. Glorify Messiah! Amen.

[Jesus to his followers] You are the light of the world.

MATTHEW 5:14A NIV

DAY (30)

Jesus blesses me with his Light when he ....

....

....

....

....

....

....

....

....

....

✦————— PRAYER OF GRATITUDE —————✦

Today, I'm thankful for ....

....

....

....

....

....

....

....

....

....

Date _____

JESUS' PROMISE - NO SEPARATION BETWEEN YOU AND HOLY GOD

God protected Moses in the cleft of a rock on
Mount Sinai to allow him to experience the
Father's Glory indirectly. But you, a saved
believer in Jesus, can experience the
Father's Glory shining directly from the
Son's face with no separation of temple curtain.
Praise God for welcoming you, the unfit, into
his presence based on the perfection of
Jesus' Light of Righteousness. Amen.

*All of us who have had the veil removed can see
and reflect the glory of the Lord. And the Lord —
who is the Spirit — makes us more and more like
him as we are changed into his glorious image.*

2 CORINTHIANS 3:18 NLT

Thank you, God, in Jesus' name that he shares
his Light with me, which make me acceptable to
you through his own divine worthiness. Amen.

*For though once your heart was full of darkness,
now it is full of light from the Lord.*

EPHESIANS 5:8A TLB

✦ ——— HEART THOUGHTS ———✦

Jesus blesses me with his Light when he ....

....

....

....

....

....

....

....

....

....

✦ ——— PRAYER OF GRATITUDE ———✦

Today, I'm thankful for ....

....

....

....

....

....

....

....

....

Date _____

JESUS' LIGHT -
GOD'S ABSOLUTE DOMINION

Your Heavenly Father exercises his authority
over light and dark to showcase his sovereignty
and goodness. Rejoice in his righteous arm!

*The Word (Jesus) was first, the Word present to God,
God present to the Word. The Word was God,
in readiness for God from day one. Everything was
created through him; nothing — not one thing! —
came into being without him. What came into
existence was Life, and the Life was Light to live by.
The Life-Light blazed out of the darkness;
and the darkness could not put it out.*

JOHN 1:1-5 MSG

Thank you, God, in Jesus' name for making me
a part of 1 THESSALONIANS 5:5A ESV *For you are all
children of light, children of the day (saved in Jesus).*
Amen.

*[God] I will turn the darkness into light before
them and make the rough places smooth.*

ISAIAH 42:16B NIV

DAY (32)

Jesus blesses me with his Light when he ....

....

....

....

....

....

....

....

....

....

————— PRAYER OF GRATITUDE —————

Today, I'm thankful for ....

....

....

....

....

....

....

....

....

....

Date _____

IRRESISTIBLY ATTRACTED TO JESUS' LIGHT - GOD'S WILL FOR YOU!

Praise your Heavenly Father for drawing you toward him by the power of Jesus' own Radiance. Oh, Son in the Holy Trinity, wholly God Yourself, Light within the Holy Spirit - shine on me! Amen.

Long ago, at many times and in many ways, God spoke to our fathers by the prophets, but in these last days, he has spoken to us by his Son, whom he appointed heir of all things, through whom also he created the world. He is the radiance of the glory of God and the exact imprint of his nature, and he upholds the universe by the word of his power.

HEBREWS 1:1-3A ESV

Jesus, in your name use me as a ray of your healing Light of Life to bless others. Amen.

For as the Father has life in himself, so he has granted the Son also to have life in himself.

JOHN 5:26 NIV

DAY (33)

HEART THOUGHTS

Jesus blesses me with his Light when he ....

....

....

....

....

....

....

....

....

....

PRAYER OF GRATITUDE

Today, I'm thankful for ....

....

....

....

....

....

....

....

....

....

Date _____

RECONCILIATION IN JESUS' LIGHT

God's flame of virtue – *JESUS!* – released you
from the death grip of sin's darkness and
made you glow with divine effulgence.
Praise your Savior in his Light of Righteousness,
which he shared through his grace of salvation
to reconcile you with your Heavenly Father.

Open up before God, keep nothing back;
he'll do whatever needs to be done:
He'll validate your life in the clear light of day
and stamp your approval at high noon.
PSALM 37:5-6 MSG

In your name, Jesus, thank you for convicting me
of the dark absence of hope in my unrighteousness
by contrasting it with your Holy Radiance.
You - my One Bright Source of Hope -
brought me out of sin's shadow into your Light by
flooding my heart with your own luminance.
Let me reflect You, Lord! Amen.

Christ lives in you.
This gives you assurance of sharing his glory.
COLOSSIANS 1:27B NLT

HEART THOUGHTS

Jesus blesses me with his Light when he ....

....

....

....

....

....

....

....

....

....

PRAYER OF GRATITUDE

Today, I'm thankful for ....

....

....

....

....

....

....

....

....

....

Date _____

BRIGHT IN YOUR SAVIOR, SAVED IN HIS LIGHT

Since righteousness is Light in God's lexicon, you
began increasing in your Father's righteousness
when your Savior transformed you. He made you
into a new Spirit-filled, Light-filled creature
for you had no light of your own. He saved you!

You were once darkness, but now you are light in the
Lord; walk as children of light (for the fruit of the light
consists of all goodness, righteousness, and truth),
as you try to learn what is pleasing to the Lord.
EPHESIANS 5:8-10 NASB

Thank you, God, in Jesus' name for your
promise in **PROVERBS 13:9A** *The light of the righteous*
shines brightly. Glory to you, Father, for making me
pure in my Savior as I am impure on my own.
I am now covered by his Light of Righteousness,
which means I can pray directly to you,
Holy Father, through your Son's worthiness.
Jesus' goodness is perfect! Praise his name! Amen.

Light shines on the righteous
and joy on the upright in heart.
PSALM 97:11 NIV

✦ ———— HEART THOUGHTS ———— ✦

Jesus blesses me with his Light when he ....

....

....

....

....

....

....

....

....

....

✦ ———— PRAYER OF GRATITUDE ———— ✦

Today, I'm thankful for ....

....

....

....

....

....

....

....

....

....

Date _____

Jesus' Light - God's Daybreak

As dawn blooms each morning, thank your
Heavenly Father for his mercy. He is faithful!

*The steadfast love of the LORD never ceases;
his mercies never come to an end; they are new
every morning; great is your faithfulness.*
Lamentations 3:22-23 ESV

Dear God, I am grateful that when my sinful
heart aches with remorse and repentance, you
never fail to answer my prayers for forgiveness.
You wash my sins away with Jesus' blood,
and like a hopeful new daybreak, you renew
my relationship with merciful You! *Weeping may
tarry for the night, but joy comes with the morning.*
Psalm 30:5b KJV
In my Savior's faithful name, amen.

*Cause me to hear thy lovingkindness in the morning;
for in thee do I trust: cause me to know the way
wherein I should walk; for I lift up my soul unto thee.*
Psalm 143:8 KJV

❖——— HEART THOUGHTS ———❖

Jesus blesses me with his Light when he ....

....

....

....

....

....

....

....

....

....

❖——— PRAYER OF GRATITUDE ———❖

Today, I'm thankful for ....

....

....

....

....

....

....

....

....

....

Date _____

GOD'S ORIGINAL
YULETIDE LIGHT - JESUS!

Next time you enjoy a Christmas tree's twinkling
lights, remember God's gift of Jesus' divine Light
that arrived in the world at his birth. Recall also
your rebirth in Him when he infused you
with the Truth Light of His Holy Spirit
at your salvation.

*O Christmas tree, O Christmas tree, What golden
lights adorn thee! Like stars they shine in
beauty bright, To fill each heart with pure delight.
O Christmas tree, O Christmas tree,
What golden lights adorn thee!*

GERMAN FOLK SONG

Thank you, God, in Jesus' name that the
star-shaped light topping my Christmas tree
is reminiscent of Jesus' Truth Light, and the
smaller lights on the lower branches represent
his worshiping saints. Let me be among those
lesser lights praising the Son's Light of Love.
Amen.

*The leaves of the tree (of life) were
for the healing of the nations.*

REVELATION 22:2B ESV

✦ —— HEART THOUGHTS —— ✦

Jesus blesses me with his Light when he ....

....

....

....

....

....

....

....

....

....

✦ —— PRAYER OF GRATITUDE —— ✦

Today, I'm thankful for ....

....

....

....

....

....

....

....

....

....

Date _____

Revitalizing Properties of Jesus' Radiance

Satan tries to sicken you with his shade of death and lies, even as God in the Spirit heals you with his Light of Life and Truth. Be enlightened. Be enlivened. Seek the Spirit in Scripture. Seek Jesus!

[Jesus] The Spirit can make life. Sheer muscle and willpower don't make anything happen. Every word I have spoken to you is a Spirit-word, and so it is life-making.

John 6:63 msg

Thank you, Holy Spirit, in Jesus' name for shining your Light of Truth into my heart. I am alive in my Savior who is the Son in the Holy Trinity - Father, Son, and Spirit. Amen.

[Paul] I am remembering you in my prayers, that the God of our Lord Jesus Christ, the Father of glory, may give you the Spirit of wisdom and of revelation in the knowledge of him, having the eyes of your hearts enlightened, that you may know what is the hope to which he has called you.

Ephesians 1:16b-18a esv

✦ ——————— HEART THOUGHTS ——————— ✦

Jesus blesses me with his Light when he ....

....

....

....

....

....

....

....

....

....

✦ ——————— PRAYER OF GRATITUDE ——————— ✦

Today, I'm thankful for ....

....

....

....

....

....

....

....

....

....

Date _____

SAFE IN JESUS' LOVE LIGHT

Morning by morning your Savior reminds you
of his Spiritual dawn of salvation. Now that he
has saved you from darkness of sin, nothing can
separate you from his Light of Righteousness.

[Paul] For I am persuaded that neither death, nor life,
nor angels, nor principalities, nor powers, nor things
present, nor things to come, nor height, nor depth,
nor any other creature, shall be able to separate us
from the love of God, which is in Christ Jesus our Lord.
ROMANS 8:38-39 NLT

In your name, Jesus, thank you that the
Holy Spirit uses each fresh dawn to point my
mind toward you. How compassionate you are
to forgive and heal me through your gifts of
mercy, grace, reconciliation, and restoration.
Amen.

Morning by morning new mercies I see;
All I have needed, thy hand hath provided.
Great is thy faithfulness Lord unto me!
THOMAS CHISOLM

HEART THOUGHTS

Jesus blesses me with his Light when he ....

....

....

....

....

....

....

....

....

....

PRAYER OF GRATITUDE

Today, I'm thankful for ....

....

....

....

....

....

....

....

....

....

Date _____

WISDOM OF FATHER GOD - HIS SON'S LIGHT IN THE WORD

When Jesus saved you, God's Holy Spirit
quickened new life within your heart.
Then he began blessing you by opening your
Spiritual eyes to God's wisdom by the
Light of his Word. Claim God's promise
to enlighten you through his
Spirit's instruction in Scripture.

*[Jesus] But the Helper, the Holy Spirit,
whom the Father will send in my name, he
will teach you all things, and bring to your
remembrance all that I have said to you.*

JOHN 14:26 ESV

Thank you, Holy Spirit, for loving me enough to
fill my heart with your divine wisdom whenever
I open my *Bible* to seek God. You share with me
the mind of Christ in whose name I pray. Amen.

*And we impart this in words not taught by
human wisdom but by the Spirit, interpreting
spiritual truths to those who are spiritual.*

1 CORINTHIANS 2:13 ESV

✦ ——— HEART THOUGHTS ——— ✦

Jesus blesses me with his Light when he ....

....

....

....

....

....

....

....

....

....

✦ ——— PRAYER OF GRATITUDE ——— ✦

Today, I'm thankful for ....

....

....

....

....

....

....

....

....

....

Date _____

SPECIALLY SELECTED TO LIVE IN JESUS' LIGHT - YOUR BLESSING!

God chose you as his saved creation,
a favored light bearer for his Son. Now he
wants you to shine with Jesus' Salvation
Radiance to draw others to new life in him.
God selected you to love and be loved.

*But you are a chosen people, a royal priesthood, a
holy nation, God's particular possession, that you
may declare the praises of him (Jesus) who called
you out of darkness into his wonderful light.*

1 PETER 2:9 NIV

In your name, Jesus, thank you for God's
promise in **1 THESSALONIANS 1:4** ESV *For we know,
brothers loved by God, that he has chosen you.*
Savior, let me share your Light with others!
Amen.

*[Jesus] You did not choose me, but I chose you and
appointed you that you should go and bear fruit
and that your fruit should abide.*

JOHN 15:16A ESV

✦ ———— HEART THOUGHTS ———— ✦

Jesus blesses me with his Light when he ....

....

....

....

....

....

....

....

....

....

✦ ———— PRAYER OF GRATITUDE ———— ✦

Today, I'm thankful for ....

....

....

....

....

....

....

....

....

....

Date _____

DAY

YOU IN JESUS' RADIANCE -
GLOWING WITH VIGOR AND VERVE

God gave you natural *sun*light to meet your
physical needs and supernatural *Son*Light to
meet your Spiritual needs. Glorify Jesus
who illumines your life in every way.

*In the beginning God created the heavens and
the earth. Now the earth was formless and empty,
darkness was over the surface of the deep, and the
spirit of God was hovering over the waters. And
God said, "Let there be light," and there was light.
God saw that the light was good.*

GENESIS 1:1-4A NIV

In your Son's name, thank you, Father, for
physical light, but thank you more for Jesus'
Spiritual Light of Love and Life that is You.
Glorify my Savior's Holy Radiance! Amen.

*The same (Jesus) was in the beginning with God.
In him was life; and the life was the Light of men.
And the light shineth in darkness;
and the darkness comprehended it not.*

JOHN 1:2; 4B KJV

✦ ——— HEART THOUGHTS ——— ✦

Jesus blesses me with his Light when he ....

....

....

....

....

....

....

....

....

....

✦ ——— PRAYER OF GRATITUDE ——— ✦

Today, I'm thankful for ....

....

....

....

....

....

....

....

....

....

Date _____

DAY 43

CALLED TO SHARE JESUS' LIGHT

How do you define your personal role
in spreading the Gospel to those who
need the Son's Salvation Radiance?

There are souls to rescue, there are souls to save.
Send the light! Send the light!
Send the light, the blessed Gospel light;
Let it shine from shore to shore! Send the light,
and let its radiant beams light the world forevermore!
CHARLES GABRIEL

Thank you, Jesus, for making it clear in
Scripture that I am to shine your Gospel
Radiance of Salvation on others. In your name,
Light of the World and my Savior, I pray for
prompting from the Spirit to bear witness
of your Good News to the lost.
Speak through me, Holy Spirit! Amen.

And he (Jesus) said to them (his disciples), "As you
go into all the world, preach openly the wonderful
news of the gospel to the entire human race!"
MARK 16:15 TPT

✧ ——— HEART THOUGHTS ——— ✧

Jesus blesses me with his Light when he ....

....

....

....

....

....

....

....

....

....

✧ ——— PRAYER OF GRATITUDE ——— ✧

Today, I'm thankful for ....

....

....

....

....

....

....

....

....

....

Date _____

Jesus' Light of Truth in Prayer and the Word - Your Treasure!

God made you able to put every teacher
and teaching through two filters:
1. Your Heavenly Father's Truth in Scripture, and
2. Your own personal prayers for discernment
of God's Truth through the teaching of the
Spirit, both of which guarantee you will not
be deceived by Satan's counterfeit light
that in reality is evil's darkness.

*For Satan himself masquerades as an angel of light.
It is not surprising, then, if his servants also
masquerade as servants of righteousness.*

2 Corinthians 11:14b niv

Father, thank you in the Savior's name for
Luke 11:35 niv *See to it, then, that the light within
you is not darkness.* For Jesus' authentic Light
burns Satan's false "light" to utter ashes.
Amen.

[Jesus] I saw Satan fall like lightning from heaven.
Luke 10:18b niv

✦ ——— HEART THOUGHTS ——— ✦

Jesus blesses me with his Light when he ....

....

....

....

....

....

....

....

....

....

✦ ——— PRAYER OF GRATITUDE ——— ✦

Today, I'm thankful for ....

....

....

....

....

....

....

....

....

....

Date _____

PERFECT SPIRITUAL VISION - YOUR GIFT IN THE LIGHT OF JESUS

Just as you can open or close your physical
eyes to *sun*light, you can open or close
your Spiritual eyes to *Son*Light.
Wake up! See Jesus!

You, God, are a fountain of cascading light,
and you open our eyes to light!
PSALM 36:9 MSG

Thank you, Father, in Jesus' name for
opening my Spiritual eyes to behold him in
REVELATION 22:16 NIV: *[Jesus] I am the Root and*
offspring of David, and the bright Morning Star.
Amen.

[Jesus] Your eye is a lamp, lighting up your whole
body. If you live wide-eyed in wonder and belief,
your body fills up with light. If you live squinty-eyed
in greed and distrust, your body is a musty cellar.
Keep your eyes open and your lamp burning, so
you don't get musty and murky. Keep your life as
well-lighted as your best-lighted room.
LUKE 11:34-36 MSG

✦——— HEART THOUGHTS ———✦

Jesus blesses me with his Light when he ....

....

....

....

....

....

....

....

....

....

✦——— PRAYER OF GRATITUDE ———✦

Today, I'm thankful for ....

....

....

....

....

....

....

....

....

....

Date _____

COMPLETE CONFIDENCE IN JESUS' LIGHT - YOURS FOR THE PRAYING

As Jesus was dying on the cross, darkness enveloped the earth from noon to three. If you had been there, would you have had sufficient faith to keep on believing he was God's Son, Light of the World?

It was now about the sixth hour, and there was darkness over the whole land until the ninth hour.

LUKE 23:44 ESV

Thank you, Father, for giving me faith to know that Jesus' Light as the risen Savior dispels all shadows of sin and death. I am saved to Light, Life, and Love in Him. Glorify his name! Amen.

Suddenly two men appeared above them (the women at the open door of Jesus' tomb) in dazzling white robes shining like lightning. The men in white said to them, "Why would you look for the Living One in a tomb. He is not here. He has risen!"

LUKE 24:4B; 5B TPT

DAY 46

⟶ HEART THOUGHTS ⟶

Jesus blesses me with his Light when he ....

....

....

....

....

....

....

....

....

....

⟶ PRAYER OF GRATITUDE ⟶

Today, I'm thankful for ....

....

....

....

....

....

....

....

....

....

Date _____

Immutability of God's Light in Jesus - Changeless and True

Be grateful the God-Spirit-Light
of the Old Testament is the same
Jesus-Spirit-Light of the New Testament.

Light is sown (by God) for the righteous,
and gladness for the upright in heart.

Psalm 97:11 KJV

Thank you, Father, that when you saved me in
Jesus, you sowed your Light in my heart through
the regenerating power of the Holy Spirit.
In Jesus' name, I pray to remain filled with the
Spirit, embodying the Son's Light to share with
others. I pray in His Refulgent Name. Amen.

[Jesus] I am the light of the world.
Whoever follows me will not walk in darkness,
but will have the light of life."

John 8:12b ESV

[Jesus, speaking to believers]
You are the light of the world.

Matthew 5:14a NIV

✦——— HEART THOUGHTS ———✦

Jesus blesses me with his Light when he ....

....

....

....

....

....

....

....

....

....

✦——— PRAYER OF GRATITUDE ———✦

Today, I'm thankful for ....

....

....

....

....

....

....

....

....

....

Date _____

Free to Live in Jesus' Radiance

When you feel chained and hopeless, go to
ACTS 12 and consider how God's angel, glowing
with celestial light, entered Peter's jail cell in a dark
Roman prison. The angel woke Peter and caused
his chains to fall away. Then he freed him
from execution into freedom's light.

[Peter] Now I know without a doubt that the Lord has
sent his angel and rescued me from Herod's clutches.
ACTS 12:11B NIV

Savior, you liberated me from sin's
dark prison into your Light. In your name,
I pray, praise, and worship you in the
Holy Trinity - Father, Son, and Holy Spirit!
Amen.

He (God) delivered us from the power of darkness and
transferred us to the Kingdom of the Son he loves.
COLOSSIANS 1:13 NET

✦——— HEART THOUGHTS ———✦

Jesus blesses me with his Light when he ....

....

....

....

....

....

....

....

....

....

✦——— PRAYER OF GRATITUDE ———✦

Today, I'm thankful for ....

....

....

....

....

....

....

....

....

....

Date _____

Jesus' Radiance - God's Reservoir of Wisdom

If you want to please your Father, ask the Spirit
to bless you with wisdom as you pray and study
the Word in Scripture and the Word in Jesus.

*For you were once darkness, but now you are light in
the Lord. Live as children of light (for the fruit of the
light consists of all goodness, righteousness,
and truth) and find out what pleases the Lord.
Have nothing to do with fruitless deeds of darkness,
but rather expose them.*

Ephesians 5:8-11 niv

Father, let me please you by rejecting Satan's
darkness and embracing your Light.
Jesus is my model, Scripture my instruction,
and the Holy Spirit my teacher.
I pray in Messiah's name. Amen.

*Do not gloat over me, my enemy! Though I have
fallen, I will rise. Though I sit in darkness,
the LORD will be my light.*

Micah 7:8 niv

✦ —————— HEART THOUGHTS —————— ✦

Jesus blesses me with his Light when he ....

....

....

....

....

....

....

....

....

....

✦ —————— PRAYER OF GRATITUDE —————— ✦

Today, I'm thankful for ....

....

....

....

....

....

....

....

....

....

Date _____

Overflowing with Jesus' Radiance - Your Delight!

Only God in his Holy Trinity – Father, Son, and Holy Spirit, source of all physical and spiritual Light of Life – can infuse you by the power of God with the eternal Life Light of Jesus, our Father's Word.

For you have delivered my soul from death,
yes, my feet from falling,
that I may walk before God in the light of life.
Psalm 56:13 esv

Father, I pray my gratitude for your eternal Life Light, your gift to me when Jesus paid my sin debt with his own spilled blood, thereby saving my soul. Thank you, God, in His Radiant Name! Amen.

In him (Jesus) was life,
and the life was the light of men.
John 1:4 esv

✦ ——————— HEART THOUGHTS ——————— ✦

Jesus blesses me with his Light when he ....

....

....

....

....

....

....

....

....

....

✦ ——————— PRAYER OF GRATITUDE ——————— ✦

Today, I'm thankful for ....

....

....

....

....

....

....

....

....

....

Date _____

DAY 51

GOODNESS OF GOD - BEAUTY AND BOUNTY WITHIN JESUS' RADIANCE

If you have the Light of Goodness shining
forth from your heart, never think it
originates with you. True goodness is a
fruit of the indwelling Holy Spirit who
regenerated you at your salvation.

Don't hide your light! Let it shine for all;
let your good deeds glow for all to see,
so that they will praise your Heavenly Father.
MATTHEW 5:15-16 TLB

Thank you, God, for shining Jesus'
righteousness on unworthy me. Your Spirit
indwelled me at my salvation and now
guides me in the Savior's uprightness,
even as I fail so often in my own weakness.
In Jesus' name of forgiving grace, I pray to
shine his Light of Goodness on others. Amen.

We must live honorably, surrounded
by the light (Jesus!) of this new day.
ROMANS 14:13A TPT

✦ ——— HEART THOUGHTS ——— ✦

Jesus blesses me with his Light when he ....

....

....

....

....

....

....

....

....

....

✦ ——— PRAYER OF GRATITUDE ——— ✦

Today, I'm thankful for ....

....

....

....

....

....

....

....

....

....

Date _____

Faithfulness in Suffering - Loyalty to Jesus in His Light

Unwavering faith during periods of your own suffering may be the only Light of Jesus some lost person will ever see.

Rejoice insofar as you share Christ's sufferings that you may also rejoice and be glad when his glory (Light!) is revealed.

1 Peter 4:13 esv

Father, I pray in Jesus' name that during my times of woe, faith in him will increase, for I believe increased faith makes the Spirit Light of your Son - the Holy Spirit inside my heart - burn brighter toward others. Make my testimony hopeful whenever I suffer so that the Spirit will use my faithfulness to witness for Jesus. Amen.

For I consider that the sufferings of this present time are not worth comparing with the glory that is to be revealed to us.

Romans 8:18 esv

✦ ———— HEART THOUGHTS ———— ✦

Jesus blesses me with his Light when he ....

....

....

....

....

....

....

....

....

....

✦ ———— PRAYER OF GRATITUDE ———— ✦

Today, I'm thankful for ....

....

....

....

....

....

....

....

....

....

Date _____

LITERAL AND METAPHORICAL LIGHT OF JESUS - BOTH REAL!

James refers to God in Holy Scripture as the
Father of Lights in the plural, even as John
declares God's Light in the singular.
Do you think the word, Light, in both phrases
goes beyond the metaphorical meaning of
God's goodness to the literal meaning
of his actual Glory Light?

*[Paul] He (God) alone can never die, and he lives in
light so brilliant that no human can approach him.
No human eye has ever seen him, nor ever will.
All honor and power to him forever! Amen.*

1 TIMOTHY 6:16 NLT

Thank you, Heavenly Father, in Jesus'
name for sharing the splendor of
your Glory Light in the Life of your Son.
He is the radiance of the glory of God.
HEBREWS 1:3A ESV. Amen.

*God is light, pure light;
there's not a trace of darkness in him.*

1 JOHN 1:5B MSG

← ———— HEART THOUGHTS ————— ←

Jesus blesses me with his Light when he ....

....

....

....

....

....

....

....

....

....

← ———— PRAYER OF GRATITUDE ————— ←

Today, I'm thankful for ....

....

....

....

....

....

....

....

....

....

Date _____

DAY 54

No Room for Human Anger in Jesus' Divine Radiance

Nurtured anger leads your heart toward darkness instead of Light. Heed the Holy Spirit's instruction in God's Word - *Do not let the sun go down while you are still angry, and do not give the devil a foothold.* Ephesians 4:26b-27 niv

Lead with your ears, follow up with your tongue, and let anger straggle along in the rear. God's righteousness does not grow from human anger.
James 1:19b-20 msg

Father, thank you in Jesus' name for wise counsel in Scripture concerning anger. I need your intervention to turn my tendency toward a bad temper into your willingness to forgive. Help me, God! Amen.

Bridle your anger, trash your wrath, cool your pipes. Anger makes things worse.
Psalm 37:8 msg

DAY (54)

✦ ———— **HEART THOUGHTS** ———— ✦

Jesus blesses me with his Light when he ....

....

....

....

....

....

....

....

....

....

✦ ———— **PRAYER OF GRATITUDE** ———— ✦

Today, I'm thankful for ....

....

....

....

....

....

....

....

....

....

Date _____

Divine Truth - God's Language and Subject Matter within Jesus' Radiance

What have you chosen to fuel your speech –
Satan's inauthentic light of understanding
(deception and evil), or God's authentic
Light of Understanding (Truth and Goodness).

*The tongue is also a fire, a world of evil among
the parts of the body. It corrupts the whole body,
sets the whole course of one's life on fire,
and is itself set on fire by hell.*

James 3:6 NIV

Father, in Jesus' name thank you for
His divine authority to speak
your Truth. Amen.

The unfolding of your words gives light.

Psalm 119:130a NIV

Whatever is in the heart overflows into speech.

Luke 6:45b TLB

✦ ———— HEART THOUGHTS ———— ✦

Jesus blesses me with his Light when he ....

....

....

....

....

....

....

....

....

....

✦ ———— PRAYER OF GRATITUDE ———— ✦

Today, I'm thankful for ....

....

....

....

....

....

....

....

....

....

Date _____

Condition of Your Saved Soul - Glowing with the Radiance of Jesus

When Jesus shone his divine refulgence on you
at the moment of your salvation, he caused
you to beam with his own saving Light.

*[Paul] In these last days, he (God) spoke to us through
his Son (Jesus), whom he made heir of all things and
through whom he created the universe, who is the
refulgence of his glory, the very imprint of his being,
and who sustains all things by his mighty word.*

Hebrews 1:2-3a nabre

In your name, Jesus, I thank Edward Plumptre for
his inspired words about your divine refulgence –
*O Light, whose beams illumine all,
from twilight dawn to perfect day, shine thou before
the shadows fall that lead our wandering feet astray.*
Savior Light, lead me to YOU! Amen.

*As we obey God's commandment to love one another,
the darkness in our lives disappears and
new light of life in Christ shines in.*

1 John 2:8b tlb

❧ ———— HEART THOUGHTS ————— ❧

Jesus blesses me with his Light when he ....

....

....

....

....

....

....

....

....

....

❧ ———— PRAYER OF GRATITUDE ————— ❧

Today, I'm thankful for ....

....

....

....

....

....

....

....

....

....

Date _____

Salvation in Jesus' Radiance - Your Unmerited Gift from God

God broke heaven's dawn upon you when he
saved you by his Son's Light, for Jesus is
worthy in his holy perfection to purify your life
with his ultimate Light Source of Agape Love.

*The light of God's love shone within us when
he sent his matchless Son into the world,
so that we might live through him.*

1 John 4:9 tpt

Thank you, God, in the name of Jesus for
shining his Light of Love on me by the power of
the Holy Spirit...all before you ever created me.
Amen.

*[Zacharias] God's love and kindness will shine upon
us like the sun that rises in the sky. On us who live in
the dark shadow of death, this Light (prophecy of Jesus)
will shine to guide us into a life of peace.*

Luke 1:78-79 cev

✦ —— HEART THOUGHTS —— ✦

Jesus blesses me with his Light when he ....

....
....
....
....
....
....
....
....
....

✦ —— PRAYER OF GRATITUDE —— ✦

Today, I'm thankful for ....

....
....
....
....
....
....
....
....
....

Date _____

LIGHT OF RELIABILITY IN GOD'S PROPHECIES - PERFECT AND TRUE

Out of his deep love for you, your Heavenly
Father has fulfilled, and continues to fulfill,
every detail of his Scriptural prophecies
concerning Messiah Jesus,
His Holy Son and Divine Radiance.

A Star shall come out of Jacob;
a Sceptre shall rise out of Israel.

NUMBERS 24:17B KJV

Thank you, God, for inspiring your prophets
to foretell Jesus' birth. In his name, accept my
gratitude for Salvation Light in your Son.
Glorify his Resplendence that is YOU!
Amen.

We also have the prophetic message as something
completely reliable, and you will do well to pay
attention to it, as to a light shining in a dark
place, until the day dawns and the morning star
(Jesus) rises in your hearts.

2 PETER 1:19 NIV

DAY 58

── **Heart Thoughts** ──

Jesus blesses me with his Light when he ....

....

....

....

....

....

....

....

....

....

── **Prayer of Gratitude** ──

Today, I'm thankful for ....

....

....

....

....

....

....

....

....

....

Date _____

DAY (59)

GOD'S HOLINESS WITHIN JESUS' LIGHT - EXQUISITELY MANIFESTED

God is love, and God loves. God is Light,
and God Lights. God is life, and God quickens life.
God is holy, and God sanctifies.
God is Creator, and God creates. God is perfect,
and God perfects. God is owner of everything,
and God shares. God is good,
and God conquers evil. God is the Father, Spirit,
and Son Jesus - the Holy One who saved you
from sin and death by his Light of Love.

*For in him (Jesus) the whole fullness
of deity dwells bodily.*

COLOSSIANS 2:9 ESV

In your name, thank you, Savior, that you
embody the deific nature of Father God
and also the Holy Spirit in your Light of Love,
Life, and Salvation. You saved me,
because you loved me! Amen.

*But Christ proved God's passionate love for us by
dying in our place while we were lost and ungodly.*

ROMANS 5:8 TPT

✦——— HEART THOUGHTS ———✦

Jesus blesses me with his Light when he ....

....

....

....

....

....

....

....

....

....

✦——— PRAYER OF GRATITUDE ———✦

Today, I'm thankful for ....

....

....

....

....

....

....

....

....

....

Date _____

FLOW OF JESUS' LIGHT FROM YOUR HEART TO OTHERS - UNCEASING!

Shekhinah can be defined as a house or dwelling place like the tent tabernacle in the Old Testament from which God's Shekhinah Glory shone. For that is what Scripture teaches that you become when you give your heart to Christ – a living temple, a clean abode for the Holy Spirit – from which the Radiance of God in Jesus will shine his Love Light from your heart toward others.

Do you not know that you are a temple of God and the Spirit of God dwells in you?
1 CORINTHIANS 3:16 NASB

Thank you, Father, in Jesus' name for sharing your unseeable glory from within his being…
the light of knowledge of the glory of God in the face of Jesus Christ. **2 CORINTHIANS 4:6B ESV.** Amen.

When Christ, who is our life appears, you also will appear with him in glory.
COLOSSIANS 3:4 NIV

✦ ——— HEART THOUGHTS ———— ✦

Jesus blesses me with his Light when he ....

....

....

....

....

....

....

....

....

....

✦ ——— PRAYER OF GRATITUDE ——— ✦

Today, I'm thankful for ....

....

....

....

....

....

....

....

....

....

Date _____

SAFETY WITHIN JESUS' RADIANCE - GOD'S GUARANTEE

Jesus is your Savior and Protector, for even as he pours his Holy Light upon you extravagantly, he also shields you from what you cannot bear of the Father's burning brilliance. The Son in the Godhead - Father, Son, and Holy Spirit - is your Shepherd Jesus, wholly God Himself who saves and keeps you.

The LORD watches over you! The LORD stands beside you as your protective shade. The sun will not harm you by day, nor the moon at night.

PSALM 121:5-6 NLT

Thank you, God, in your Son's name that he watches over me. I flourish in Jesus' perfect level of intensity within his Life Light. He is my Savior! Amen.

My dear children, I write this to you so that you will not sin. But if anyone does sin, we have an advocate (protector) with the Father - Jesus Christ, the Righteous One.

1 JOHN 2:1 NIV

HEART THOUGHTS

Jesus blesses me with his Light when he ....

....

....

....

....

....

....

....

....

....

PRAYER OF GRATITUDE

Today, I'm thankful for ....

....

....

....

....

....

....

....

....

....

Date _____

ACCEPTING JESUS' LIGHT OF SALVATION - YOUR GLAD CHOICE!

You cannot linger in some twilight neutrality
between a decision to - or not to - ask Jesus to
forgive your sins and save you by his grace.
God breaks down your decision requirement
distinctly. You may choose to be *for* Jesus in
his Light or *against* him in Satan's darkness.
No in-between.

Whoever believes in him (Jesus) is not condemned,
but whoever does not believe is condemned already,
because he has not believed in the
name of the Son of God.

JOHN 3:18 ESV

In your name, thank you, Jesus, for calling me to
choose your divine Light of Life and reject Satan's
deadly darkness. I have decided for YOU! Amen.

Everyone who makes a practice of doing evil,
addicted to denial and illusion, hates God-light
and won't come near it. But anyone working and
living in truth and reality welcomes God-light (Jesus).

JOHN 3:20-21A MSG

✦——— HEART THOUGHTS ———✦

Jesus blesses me with his Light when he ....

....

....

....

....

....

....

....

....

....

✦——— PRAYER OF GRATITUDE ———✦

Today, I'm thankful for ....

....

....

....

....

....

....

....

....

....

Date _____

Choosing Jesus' Light of Love

Love and enlighten are verbs that belong to
Jesus, while hate and darken belong to Satan.
Jesus wants to love and bless others through
you as he Lights your way toward life in him.
Satan wants to do the opposite. Reject Satan
and choose Jesus for he is the healing
Radiance you need. Your Savior loves you
and wants you to love him in return.

*Again, Jesus spoke to them, saying, "I am the light
of the world. Whoever follows me will not walk in
darkness but will have the light of life."*

John 8:12 esv

Thank you, Jesus, for lighting my path. In your
name, let me share your Love, Light, and Life
with others as I claim your promise in **John 15:9 nlt:**
*I have loved you even as the Father has loved me.
Remain in my love.* Amen.

*For he has rescued us out of the darkness and
gloom of Satan's kingdom and brought us into
the Kingdom of his dear Son.*

Colossians 1:13 tlb

✦———— HEART THOUGHTS ————✦

Jesus blesses me with his Light when he ....

....

....

....

....

....

....

....

....

....

✦———— PRAYER OF GRATITUDE ————✦

Today, I'm thankful for ....

....

....

....

....

....

....

....

....

....

Date _____

SECURITY IN JESUS' RADIANCE - YOUR SAFE ZONE

Have no fear of those living in rebellion against God's Light. Jesus will help you defend yourself with his own Glory in the face of Satan's gloom. Claim your Heavenly Father's Scriptural promise with bold confidence: *[Paul] If God is for us, who can ever be against us?* **ROMANS 8:31B NLT**

There are those who rebel against the light; they do not know its ways, and they do not stay on its paths. The morning to them is like deep darkness; they are friends with the terrors of darkness.

JOB 24:13; 17B NET

Heavenly Father, thank you for Jesus' willingness and authority to defend me against evil. In his name, I pray. Amen.

The Lord is my light and my salvation – whom shall I fear? The lord is the stronghold of my life - of whom shall I be afraid?

PSALM 27:1 NIV

✦ ——— HEART THOUGHTS ——— ✦

Jesus blesses me with his Light when he ....

....

....

....

....

....

....

....

....

....

✦ ——— PRAYER OF GRATITUDE ——— ✦

Today, I'm thankful for ....

....

....

....

....

....

....

....

....

....

Date _____

Blessing Others with Jesus' Light of Kindness - Your Joy!

What is your default mode as you relate to family and friends - wallowing in complaints in the enemy's shadow or seeking solutions in Christ's Light?

Do all things without grumbling or disputing, that you may be blameless and innocent, children of God without blemish in the midst of a crooked and twisted generation, among whom you shine as lights in the world, holding fast to the word of life.

Philippians 2:14-16a esv

Thank you, Father, that Jesus shone his Light of Kindness on undeserving me. In his name, I pray for strength from the indwelling Holy Spirit to emulate my Savior as I relate to others. Let them be safe in your Son's Light, not lost in Satan's darkness. Witness! Amen.

Friends, don't complain about each other. A far greater complaint could be lodged against you, you know. The Judge (Jesus at his second coming) is just around the corner.

James 5:9 msg

✦ ——— HEART THOUGHTS ———✦

Jesus blesses me with his Light when he ....

....

....

....

....

....

....

....

....

....

✦ ——— PRAYER OF GRATITUDE ———✦

Today, I'm thankful for ....

....

....

....

....

....

....

....

....

....

Date _____

NO SPACE FOR COVETOUSNESS IN JESUS' RADIANCE - ZERO! NIL!

Satan coveted God's exclusive right to be worshiped, the sin for which he was thrown out of Heaven. He still practices the same offense today, the reason God changed his name from Daystar (light) to Father of Lies (darkness). It makes sense then that your Heavenly Father addressed covetousness in the Ten Commandments of the Old Testament, *"Thou shall not covet..."* EXODUS 20:17A KJV, and Jesus addressed covetousness in the New Testament, *"Take care, and be on your guard against all covetousness..."* LUKE 12:15A ESV. Which have you chosen as your life's fulcrum, evil's darkness of covetousness or Jesus' Light of Generosity?

Thank you, God, for reminding me that envy is dark, not light. In Jesus' name, I pray for the Holy Spirit's wisdom and help in rejecting covetousness. Amen.

[Jesus] ...coveting, wickedness, deceit, sensuality, envy, slander, pride, foolishness. All these evil things come from within, and they defile a person.

MARK 7:22-23 ESV

→ ——————— **HEART THOUGHTS** ——————— ←

Jesus blesses me with his Light when he ....

....

....

....

....

....

....

....

....

....

→ ——————— **PRAYER OF GRATITUDE** ——————— ←

Today, I'm thankful for ....

....

....

....

....

....

....

....

....

....

Date _____

Glorifying God in Jesus' Light - Your Reason for Living

God enlightened you with his own
Radiance of Love and Life on the day he saved
you in Jesus. When you said, "Yes," to your
Savior - Son in the Holy Trinity...Father, Son, and
Holy Spirit - you realized with stunning clarity
that God gave you life to glorify himself.
The purpose of your existence is to magnify
your Creator in praise and worship.

[Father] Bring all who claim me as their God,
for I have made them for my glory.
It was I who created them.

Isaiah 43:7 nlt

Thank you, God, for salvation in Jesus, whom I
glorify as I glorify You - the Father and Spirit. In the
Son's luminous name, I pray my gratitude for His
saving grace. Praise and Worship Him! Amen.

Everything should be done in a way that will
bring honor to God because of Jesus Christ,
who is glorious and powerful forever. Amen.

1 Peter 4:11b cev

✦ ———— HEART THOUGHTS ————— ✦

Jesus blesses me with his Light when he ....

....

....

....

....

....

....

....

....

....

✦ ———— PRAYER OF GRATITUDE ————— ✦

Today, I'm thankful for ....

....

....

....

....

....

....

....

....

....

Date _____

DAY 68

Grace of Forgiveness in Jesus' Light - God's Gift to You

Have you ever said or done something that made
you want to hide in some shadowy corner far from
God's sight and Light? Yet you knew he wanted
to forgive you if only you would ask with
a repentant heart. Open your Spiritual ears
and listen to your Father's loving voice:
"Come back to the Light, Child. Father is calling."

*I could ask the darkness to hide me and the
light around me to become night – but even in
darkness, I cannot hide from you (God).
To you the night shines as bright as day.*
PSALM 139:11-12A NLT

In your name, Jesus, thank you that if
I stray into sin's murky regions, you remain
faithful to draw me back into your healing aura.
I am grateful to you, Radiant Savior. Amen.

*For everything that is hidden will eventually
be brought into the open, and every secret will
be brought to light. Anyone who has ears to
hear should listen and understand.*
MARK 4:22-23 NLT

DAY (68)

Jesus blesses me with his Light when he ....

....

....

....

....

....

....

....

....

....

── PRAYER OF GRATITUDE ──

Today, I'm thankful for ....

....

....

....

....

....

....

....

....

....

Date _____

LIGHT OF JESUS' TRUTH - REVEALED TO YOU BY THE SPIRIT

If you seek God in the *Bible*, the Holy Spirit will enlighten you to Spiritual understandings. Pray that he will lead you to Truth in his Word (Scripture) and Truth in his Word (Jesus), for God's ultimate Truth is your Savior.

God has let you in on the inside story regarding the workings of the Kingdom – the hidden meanings.

MARK 4:11A VOICE

Jesus, thank you for your Truth Light in Scripture. I cannot know all God's mysterious ways, but I can know what the Spirit reveals to me. I pray in your name, Jesus, the Word. Enlighten me! Amen.

When you bring a lamp into the house, do you put it under a box or stuff it under your bed? Or do you set it on top of a table or chest? Those things that are hidden are meant to be revealed, and what is concealed is meant to be brought out where its light can shine.

MARK 4:21B-22 NLT

Jesus blesses me with his Light when he ....

....

....

....

....

....

....

....

....

....

✦ ————— PRAYER OF GRATITUDE ————— ✦

Today, I'm thankful for ....

....

....

....

....

....

....

....

....

....

Date _____

Refreshment for Your Soul in Jesus' Radiance - Your Privilege

When self complains you are burned out on shining for Jesus, ask God to restore your energy. Pray for more of your Savior's Light and none of Satan's darkness. Ask the Spirit to renew your soul as you seek God in his Word. Claim Jesus' promise that *you* are Light of the World, because *He* is Light of the World. Live as Jesus' Blaze of Living Hope.

This little light of mine, I'm gonna let it shine.
This little light of mine, I'm gonna let it shine.
Don't let Satan blow it out, I'm gonna let it shine.
Let it shine! Let it shine! Let it shine!

Harry Loes

Thank you, Father, in your Son's name, for turning self's weak flicker into Jesus' powerful flame. I seek rest and salvation in him through prayer and Scripture. Renew me, Savior! Amen.

Come to me, all you who are weary and burdened, and I will give you rest.

Matthew 11:29 NIV

✦ —— HEART THOUGHTS ——✦

Jesus blesses me with his Light when he ....

....

....

....

....

....

....

....

....

....

✦ —— PRAYER OF GRATITUDE ——✦

Today, I'm thankful for ....

....

....

....

....

....

....

....

....

....

Date _____

DIVINE POWER IN JESUS' LIGHT - ALIVE, UNCREATED, HOLY

Sunlight reflected off solar sails can propel spacecrafts through the cosmos much faster than current speeds with no need of any other kind of fuel. God already knew this would be possible when he created the sun. Now if the Father can do such an amazing thing with created *sun*light, just think what he can do with uncreated *Son*Light.

Light, space, zest – that's God!
PSALM 27:1A MSG

Father, you wrap yourself in uncreated Light, just as you wrap me in Jesus' uncreated Salvation Light. In his name, thank you for his glorious Radiance. Praise you, Savior! Amen.

God's Son shines out with God's glory, and all that God's Son is and does marks him as God. He regulates the universe by the mighty power of his command.
HEBREWS 1:3A TLB

✦ ——— HEART THOUGHTS ——— ✦

Jesus blesses me with his Light when he ....

....

....

....

....

....

....

....

....

....

✦ ——— PRAYER OF GRATITUDE ——— ✦

Today, I'm thankful for ....

....

....

....

....

....

....

....

....

....

Date _____

Prayer - Your Access to Holy God in Jesus' Radiance

God commanded the Israelites to make a gold lampstand to guard the holy of holies, the special worship area shielded by a thick curtain where priests entered once a year to offer animal blood as atonement for sins. But when Jesus, God's True Lampstand, shed his own perfect blood to atone for sins of the world, he made prayer to Holy God available to all believers through his own Light of Righteousness.

Then Jesus cried out again with a loud voice and gave up his spirit. Just then the temple curtain was torn in two from top to bottom.

Matthew 27:50-51a net

In your name, Jesus, thank you for making me worthy to meet God covered by your own immaculate Light. Amen.

You may proclaim the praises of Him (Jesus) who called you out of darkness into his marvelous light.

1 Peter 2:9b nkjv

✦——— HEART THOUGHTS ———✦

Jesus blesses me with his Light when he ....

....
....
....
....
....
....
....
....
....

✦——— PRAYER OF GRATITUDE ———✦

Today, I'm thankful for ....

....
....
....
....
....
....
....
....
....

Date _____

GOD'S EXPECTATION OF YOU -
RECEIVE AND SHARE JESUS' LIGHT

God gave you his armor of Light on the day
he saved you in his Son, Jesus, who
sacrificed himself to pay your sin debt and
banish darkness from your life forever.
You are Light, because your Savior is Light.
Show him gratitude by sharing his Light
with those around you.

*[Paul] Therefore, let's rid ourselves of the deeds of
darkness and put on the armor of light. Put on the
Lord Jesus Christ and make no provision for
the flesh in regard to its lusts.*
ROMANS 13:12B; 14 NASB

Thank you, Father, in Jesus' name.
*For you have rescued us out of the
darkness and gloom of Satan's kingdom
and brought us into the Kingdom of
your dear Son.* **COLOSSIANS 1:13 TLB.** Amen.

*For we wrestle not against flesh and blood,
but against principalities, against powers,
against the rulers of the darkness of this world,
against wickedness in high places.*
EPHESIANS 6:12 KJV

✦ ——— HEART THOUGHTS ——— ✦

Jesus blesses me with his Light when he ....

....

....

....

....

....

....

....

....

....

✦ ——— PRAYER OF GRATITUDE ——— ✦

Today, I'm thankful for ....

....

....

....

....

....

....

....

....

....

Date _____

JESUS' RADIANCE -
GOD'S SALVATION LIGHT FOR YOU!

Jesus is your lantern, compass, and map to
salvation. Old Testament PSALMS point to him
as God's One and Only Son who will gladden
your heart and make you thankful for his
willingness to rescue you from sin and death.

*[Prayer to Father God] Give me your lantern and
compass, give me your map, so that I can find my way
to the sacred mountain, to the place of your presence.*

PSALM 43:3A MSG

Thank you, Jesus, for being my lantern to show
me the one path to Truth and Life. In your name
I pray my gratitude that you guide me by
the Holy Spirit. *For you are my lamp,
O LORD; and the LORD illumines my darkness.*
2 SAMUEL 22:29 NASB 1995. Amen.

*We have the prophetic words more fully confirmed,
to which you will do well to pay attention as to a
lamp shining in a dark place, until the day dawns
and the morning star (Jesus) rises in your hearts.*

2 PETER 1:19 ESV

HEART THOUGHTS

Jesus blesses me with his Light when he ....

....

....

....

....

....

....

....

....

....

PRAYER OF GRATITUDE

Today, I'm thankful for ....

....

....

....

....

....

....

....

....

....

Date _____

MARVELS AND MIRACLES IN JESUS' RADIANCE...GOD-POWER!

If God created your physical body to maintain health by producing vitamin D in response to natural sunlight, consider what he can do for your Spiritual life with his own uncreated supernatural Light, Jesus - His perfect Son and your Protector, Healer, and Savior.

If I were to say, "Certainly the darkness will cover me, and the light will turn to night all around me," even the darkness is not too dark for you (God) to see, and the night is as bright as day; darkness and light are the same to you. Certainly, you made my mind and heart; you wove me together in my mother's womb.

PSALM 139:11-13 NET

Thank you, Father, in your Son's radiant name for creating, healing, and saving me in HIM! Amen.

[Jesus] I am the world's Light. No one who follows me stumbles around in darkness. I provide plenty of light to live in.

JOHN 8:12B MSG

✦——— HEART THOUGHTS ———✦

Jesus blesses me with his Light when he ....

....

....

....

....

....

....

....

....

....

✦——— PRAYER OF GRATITUDE ———✦

Today, I'm thankful for ....

....

....

....

....

....

....

....

....

....

Date _____

LIGHT OF JESUS -
EVER BURNING, EVER BLAZING!

In the Old Covenant, as priests sacrificed
animals in atonement for sins, God the Father
instructed them never to let the altar fire go out.
This foreshadowed the New Covenant
embodied in Jesus - Son and Messiah Light
whom the Father sent to die as his unblemished
sacrifice to atone for sins of believers,
once and for all.

*Then Moses and Aaron went into the Tabernacle,
and when they came back out, they blessed the
people again, and the glory of the
Lord appeared to the whole community.*
LEVITICUS 9:23 NLT

Thank you, Father, in your Son's name for his
ultimate offering to pay my sin debt. He gave me
his sublime Light of Salvation. I am saved in Jesus
and indwelled by the Spirit. Praise God! Amen.

*[Jesus] So if you follow me, you won't be stumbling
through darkness, for living light will flood your path.*
JOHN 8:12B TLB

DAY (76)

Jesus blesses me with his Light when he ....

....

....

....

....

....

....

....

....

....

✦ ——————— **PRAYER OF GRATITUDE** ——————— ✦

Today, I'm thankful for ....

....

....

....

....

....

....

....

....

....

Date _____

ONCE YOU WERE BLIND, BUT NOW YOU CAN SEE - BY JESUS' LIGHT!

Jesus' Glory blazed so brightly before Paul on his way to Damascus that it blinded him for a time. Then God sent Ananias to help him recover, for the Father had chosen Paul for his instrument.

[Ananias] The Lord Jesus, who appeared to you on the road, has sent me so that you might regain your sight and be filled with the Holy Spirit. Instantly, something like scales fell from Paul's eyes, and he regained his sight. Then he got up and was baptized.

ACTS 9:17B-18 NLT

In your name, Savior, thank you that your awesome Light got Paul's attention. His violence toward believers had made him so dark with sin that he was overcome physically, blinded even by your Glory. And yet you chose him as your special witness. Savior Jesus, choose me! Amen.

Saul (Paul) stayed with the apostles and went all around Jerusalem with them, preaching boldly in the name of the Lord.

ACTS 9:28 NLT

DAY (77)

→ ———— HEART THOUGHTS ———— →

Jesus blesses me with his Light when he ....

....

....

....

....

....

....

....

....

....

→ ———— PRAYER OF GRATITUDE ———— →

Today, I'm thankful for ....

....

....

....

....

....

....

....

....

....

Date _____

DAY 78

JESUS - GOD'S SONLIGHT FOR YOU!

Look forward to Jesus taking you home
where he will reveal everything he has prepared
for your eternal life within his Radiance.

*We don't yet see things clearly. We're squinting
in a fog, peering through a mist. But it won't be long
before the weather clears, and the sun shines bright!
We'll see it all then, see it all as clearly as God sees us,
knowing him directly just as he knows us!*
1 CORINTHIANS 13:12 MSG

Thank you, Father, for Jesus, your gift of Light
and Life. I thrive in his shining Spirit today,
even as I anticipate eternity in his presence,
an endless future so marvelous it dazzles my
mind with his Radiance and delights my
soul with your own Love Light. I pray my
gratitude in the Son's name. Amen.

*Turn your eyes upon Jesus. Look full in His
wonderful face. And the things on earth will grow
strangely dim in the light of His glory and grace.*
HELEN LEMMEL

✦——— HEART THOUGHTS ———✦

Jesus blesses me with his Light when he ....

....

....

....

....

....

....

....

....

....

✦——— PRAYER OF GRATITUDE ———✦

Today, I'm thankful for ....

....

....

....

....

....

....

....

....

....

Date _____

SAVED AND SAFE IN JESUS' LIGHT - GOD'S SALVATION GIFT TO YOU

Fear not, believers! You have accepted Jesus as your Lord and Savior, which means you have no reason to fear evil. God Light protects you, Jesus Light advocates for you, and Spirit Light dwells within you. You are saved and safe. Fear not, believers!

[David] The LORD is my light and my salvation – why should I be afraid? The LORD is my fortress, protecting me from danger – why should I tremble?
PSALM 27:1 NLT

In your name, Jesus, thank you for helping me conquer fear. Your calm words of Light reassure me: *Let not your hearts be troubled, neither let them be afraid.* **JOHN 14:27B ESV**. Amen.

Who is he who will harm you if you follow that which is good? But even if you suffer for the sake of righteousness, you are blessed. Do not be afraid of their terror, do not be troubled, but sanctify the Lord God in your hearts.
1 PETER 3:13-15A MEV

✦ ——— HEART THOUGHTS ——— ✦

Jesus blesses me with his Light when he ....

....

....

....

....

....

....

....

....

....

✦ ——— PRAYER OF GRATITUDE ——— ✦

Today, I'm thankful for ....

....

....

....

....

....

....

....

....

....

Date _____

JESUS, THE SON - GOD'S OWN RADIANCE REVEALED TO YOU

When Jesus' returns to earth, be thankful he
will bring with him the sum total of the
Holy Trinity's Power and Glory Light –
Father, Son, and Holy Spirit. For Jesus' uncreated
Light shines through millions of divine facets
that together empower his sacred authority.
His perfection makes him worthy to share his
eternal Love, Life, and Light with you.

*And they will see the Son of man coming on the
clouds of heaven with power and great glory.*
MATTHEW 24:30B NLT

In the Savior's name, thank you, God,
for assuring me that the *Son of Man (Jesus)
is going to come with his angels in the glory
of his Father.* **MATTHEW 16:27A ESV.**
Praise him eternally! Amen.

*When Christ who is your life appears,
you will appear with him in glory.*
COLOSSIANS 3:4 ESV

✦ —————— HEART THOUGHTS —————— ✦

Jesus blesses me with his Light when he ....

....

....

....

....

....

....

....

....

....

✦ —————— PRAYER OF GRATITUDE —————— ✦

Today, I'm thankful for ....

....

....

....

....

....

....

....

....

....

Date _____

Jesus - God's Radiant Messiah, Worthy of Worship and Praise

No matter how beautiful the candles in the outer ring of the Advent wreath, they always surround and glorify the single Christ candle in the center, symbol of Jesus' Light shared with the world.

O come, Thou Dayspring, come and cheer our spirits by Thine Advent here. Disperse the gloomy clouds of night, And death's dark shadows put to flight. Rejoice! Rejoice! Emanuel shall come to thee, O Israel.

Translation by John Neale

Father, in Jesus' name, thank you for the Gospel message shining forth from the center candle of the Advent wreath. His first visit to earth as an infant gives us glad anticipation of his second coming as conquering King, for His Light Is God's Own Holy Radiance and Supremacy. Amen.

Through the tender mercy of our God; whereby the Dayspring (Jesus, the Son) from on high hath visited us.

Luke 1:78 KJV

✦——— HEART THOUGHTS ———✦

Jesus blesses me with his Light when he ....

....

....

....

....

....

....

....

....

....

✦——— PRAYER OF GRATITUDE ———✦

Today, I'm thankful for ....

....

....

....

....

....

....

....

....

....

Date _____

No More Valley of the Shadow of Death - Just Life and Safety in Your Savior's Light

Do you long to walk confidently with Jesus in his Light of Righteousness, even as you find yourself stumbling through Satan's shadow of sin? Consider the plight of the disobedient Egyptians in Moses' story and rejoice that God is in control of both light and dark. Yield to Him!

Then the Angel of God, who was leading the people of Israel, moved the cloud around behind them, and it stood between the people of Israel and the Egyptians. And that night, as it changed to a pillar of fire, it gave darkness to the Egyptians but light to the people of Israel! So the Egyptians couldn't find the Israelis!
Exodus 14:10-20 MSG

In your name, praise you, Jesus, that darkness has no power over you, which means it has no power over me. Glorify you, Savior! Amen.

For you were once darkness, but now you are Light in the Lord (Jesus).
Ephesians 5:8a ESV

✦——— HEART THOUGHTS ———✦

Jesus blesses me with his Light when he ....

....

....

....

....

....

....

....

....

....

✦——— PRAYER OF GRATITUDE ———✦

Today, I'm thankful for ....

....

....

....

....

....

....

....

....

....

Date _____

DAY 83

GRATEFUL – YOUR LOVING ATTITUDE TOWARD JESUS FOR BLESSING YOU WITH HIS LIGHT

Thank your Heavenly Father for his Light, Love, and Life in the Trinity - Father, Son, and Spirit - all of which manifest fully and eternally in Jesus, author of righteousness, worthiness, mercy, forgiveness, and grace of salvation. God's great *Son*Light shines on you!

Yours, O LORD, is the greatness and the power and the glory and the victory and the majesty, indeed, everything that is in the heavens and the earth; Yours is the dominion, O LORD, and You exalt Yourself as head over all.

1 Chronicles 29:11 nasb 1995

Thank you, Father, in Jesus' name, for making yourself relatable to me in Him, your Source of Sacred Light, Love, and Life. With all my heart, Savior Son and Lord Messiah, I trust in your declaration of your own divinity in **John 10:30 esv** *(Jesus) I and the Father are one*. Amen.

(Jesus) Anyone who has seen me has seen the Father.

John 14:9b niv

✦ —————— Heart Thoughts —————— ✦

Jesus blesses me with his Light when he ....

....

....

....

....

....

....

....

....

....

✦ —————— Prayer of Gratitude —————— ✦

Today, I'm thankful for ....

....

....

....

....

....

....

....

....

....

Date _____

DAY 84

Clear Conscience - Yours within the Purifying Light of Jesus

Only Jesus, wholly God himself, can cleanse your conscience, even as self persists in poisoning it. Thank the Father that Jesus' sinless Light with which the Spirit covered you at your salvation is what God sees when he inspects the conscience that he gave to you at your creation.

The spirit (conscience) of man is the lamp of the LORD, searching and examining all the innermost parts of his being.
PROVERBS 20:27 AMP

Thank you, Father, in Jesus' name for forgiving my sins and clearing my conscience. Amen.

Just think how much more the blood of Christ will purify our consciences from sinful deeds so that we can worship the living God. For by the power of the eternal Spirit, Christ offered himself to God as the perfect sacrifice for our sins.
HEBREWS 9:14 NLT

DAY (84)

✦ ———— **HEART THOUGHTS** ———— ✦

Jesus blesses me with his Light when he ....

....

....

....

....

....

....

....

....

....

✦ ———— **PRAYER OF GRATITUDE** ———— ✦

Today, I'm thankful for ....

....

....

....

....

....

....

....

....

....

Date _____

Foolhardiness - Not Permitted in Christ's Light of Wisdom

Do you want your mind to be brightened
by God's Truth that is wisdom,
or darkened by Satan's deceit that is folly?

Jealousy and selfishness are not God's kind of wisdom.
Such things are earthly, unspiritual, and demonic.
But the wisdom from above (God's Light of Wisdom)
is first of all pure. It is also peace-loving,
gentle at all times, and willing to yield to others.
It is full of mercy and the fruit of good deeds.
It shows no favoritism and is always sincere.

James 3:15; 17 nlt

In Jesus' name, thank you, God, for your Word
that informs my understanding of wisdom's
blessings. *Then I saw that there is more gain in*
wisdom than in folly, as there is more gain in light
than in darkness. **Ecclesiastes 2:13 esv.** Amen.

A man's wisdom illumines him
and causes his stern face to beam.

Ecclesiastes 8:1b nasb 1995

DAY 85

✦ ——— HEART THOUGHTS ———✦

Jesus blesses me with his Light when he ....

....

....

....

....

....

....

....

....

....

✦ ——— PRAYER OF GRATITUDE ———✦

Today, I'm thankful for ....

....

....

....

....

....

....

....

....

....

Date _____

DAY 86

Jesus' Light - Holy, Beautiful, Alive, Mysterious, All-Powerful!

God's Glory Light in Jesus is beautiful to the
physical eyes (inquire of Stephen and Moses),
as well as the Spiritual eyes (inquire of Zechariah).
Your Spiritual eyes are special detectors of God's
exalted goodness that lead you straight to Jesus,
your Father's sacred Branch of Living Light.

*In that day the Branch of the LORD (Jesus)
shall be beautiful and glorious.*
Isaiah 4:2 esv

Thank you, Father, in Jesus' name, that in
Stephen's dying moments as he was being stoned,
he saw Heaven open to receive him, revealing to
his suffering eyes your Light shining in all its
Glory alongside Jesus. Zechariah is also correct in
his description of your divine magnificence:
*For how great is his (God's) goodness,
and how great his beauty!* **Zechariah 9:17a kjv**
What a lovely prophetic image of Jesus'
divine Beauty Light. Amen.

From Zion, perfect in beauty, God shines forth.
Psalm 50:2 niv

✦ ─── HEART THOUGHTS ─── ✦

Jesus blesses me with his Light when he ....

....

....

....

....

....

....

....

....

....

✦ ─── PRAYER OF GRATITUDE ─── ✦

Today, I'm thankful for ....

....

....

....

....

....

....

....

....

....

Date _____

Sunlight - Unnecessary in the Presence of Jesus' SonLight

*No need of sunlight in heaven we're told; the Lamb
is the Light in the city of gold; come to the Light,
'tis shining for thee; sweetly the Light has dawned
upon me; once I was blind, but now I can see:
the Light of the World is Jesus!*

Philip Bliss

*[John, describing New Jerusalem] And the city has no
need of sun or moon to shine on it, for the Glory of
God gives it Light, and its Lamp is the Lamb (Jesus).*

Revelation 21:23 esv

In Jesus' name, thank you, God, for your Son's
healing Light revealed to me by your Spirit in
Scripture, and also through the witness of
your saints' lives. *God is light, and in him is
no darkness at all.* **1 John 1:5b kjv**. Amen.

*I, Jesus, sent my Angel to testify to these
things for the churches. I am the Root and
Branch of David, the Bright Morning Star.*

Revelation 22:16 msg

HEART THOUGHTS

Jesus blesses me with his Light when he ....

....

....

....

....

....

....

....

....

....

PRAYER OF GRATITUDE

Today, I'm thankful for ....

....

....

....

....

....

....

....

....

....

Date _____

OBEDIENCE INSPIRED BY GRATITUDE - YOUR ENLIGHTENED BEHAVIOR IN CHRIST'S RADIANCE

God gave you his commands to enhance your life, not diminish it. You will find knowledge, wisdom, and enlightenment in his statutes through obedience, and Life Light through adherence. Be liberated, never imprisoned, by your Heavenly Father's rules. And be enriched, never impoverished, by his commandments. Light up your life by submitting to God.

*The commands of the LORD are radiant,
giving light to the eyes.*
PSALM 19:8B NIV

Thank you, Father, for Jesus' perfect model of what it looks like in human behaviors and attitudes to live in obedience to your commands. In the Son's name, let me live like HIM! Amen.

*Sound advice is a beacon, good teaching a light,
and moral discipline a life path.*
PROVERBS 6:23 MSG

✦ ———— HEART THOUGHTS ————✦

Jesus blesses me with his Light when he ....

....

....

....

....

....

....

....

....

....

✦ ———— PRAYER OF GRATITUDE ————✦

Today, I'm thankful for ....

....

....

....

....

....

....

....

....

....

Date _____

DAY 89

Jesus' Expectation of You - Share His Light with Others!

Your Heavenly Father wants you to help those
around you conquer darkness by
allowing the Holy Spirit to shine God's Light
of Jesus into their hearts through you.
Blaze forth with the Radiance of your Savior!

*[God] Arise, my people! Let your light shine for
all the nations to see! For the glory of the Lord is
streaming from you. Darkness as black as night
shall cover all the peoples of the earth, but the
glory of the Lord will shine from you.*

Isaiah 60:1-3 tlb

Thank you, Savior, in your name, for leaving
Heaven to be God's Light of the World. I pray
to share your Light with everyone near me
as you so lovingly share with me. Amen.

[Jesus, about himself] I am the light of the world.

John 8:12b esv

[Jesus, about believers] You are the light of the world.

Matthew 5:14a niv

✦ ———— HEART THOUGHTS ————✦

Jesus blesses me with his Light when he ....

....

....

....

....

....

....

....

....

....

✦ ———— PRAYER OF GRATITUDE ————✦

Today, I'm thankful for ....

....

....

....

....

....

....

....

....

....

Date _____

Jesus' Holy Light - Your Eternal Hope and Assurance

God's natural light from the sun and other stars will last a finite time, but his supernatural Light that is his Spiritual Light will last forever in Himself, in the Radiance of Jesus, and in the Light of the Father and Spirit. Glorify You, Holy Trinity!

No longer will you need the sun or moon to give you light, for the Lord your God will be your everlasting light, and he will be your glory. Your sun will never set; the moon shall not go down —
for the Lord will be your everlasting light.

Isaiah 60:19-20a tlb

Thank you, God, for revealing Jesus' Light to undeserving me. The Son's purity is a blessing that helps me appreciate the everlasting nature of your goodness. In his name of Radiant Righteousness, I pray my gratitude. Amen.

He alone is immortal God, living in unapproachable light of divine glory!

1 Timothy 6:16a tpt

✦ —— HEART THOUGHTS —— ✦

Jesus blesses me with his Light when he ....

....

....

....

....

....

....

....

....

....

✦ —— PRAYER OF GRATITUDE —— ✦

Today, I'm thankful for ....

....

....

....

....

....

....

....

....

....

Date _____

NEW YOU - COVERED AND SAVED WITHIN JESUS' LIGHT, ACCEPTED AND HEARD BY HOLY GOD

The Spirit called you to Salvation in Jesus in whose Light of Righteousness, God is pleased. And if he is pleased in his Son, he is pleased in you, for Jesus covers you with his perfect Light.

[Paul] I pray that the light of God will illuminate the eyes of your imagination, flooding you with light, until you experience the full revelation of the hope of his calling – that is, the wealth of God's glorious inheritances that he finds in us, his holy ones!

EPHESIANS 1:18 TPT

In Jesus' name, thank you, God, for filling my heart with the hope of your calling in Jesus who rewarded my hope of salvation in him. Praise the Savior! Praise the Father! Praise the Holy Spirit! Amen.

Wrap your heart tightly around the hope that lives within us, knowing that God always keeps his promises!

HEBREWS 10:23B TPT

DAY (91)

✦——— HEART THOUGHTS ———✦

Jesus blesses me with his Light when he ....

....
....
....
....
....
....
....
....
....

✦——— PRAYER OF GRATITUDE ———✦

Today, I'm thankful for ....

....
....
....
....
....
....
....
....
....

Date _____

DAY 92

NATURAL LIGHT - OUR BEAUTIFUL REMINDER OF JESUS' DIVINE LIGHT

Let the created marvels of beauty light in God's sky help you remember to praise him for his own uncreated Beauty Light in Jesus Christ. Glorify your Savior!

Space itself speaks his (God's) story through the marvels of the heavens. His truth is on tour in the starry vault of the sky, showing his skill in creation's craftsmanship.

PSALM 19:1B TPT

Thank you, God, for your created light-shows in the atmosphere that shout volumes about your Living-Light-Word-Jesus, all without a spoken or written word. In his glorious name, I pray. Amen.

What a heavenly home God has set for the sun, shining in the superdome of the sky! See how it leaves its celestial chamber each morning, radiant as a bridegroom ready for his wedding, like a day-breaking champion eager to run his course.

PSALM 19:4B-5 TPT

HEART THOUGHTS

Jesus blesses me with his Light when he ....

....

....

....

....

....

....

....

....

....

PRAYER OF GRATITUDE

Today, I'm thankful for ....

....

....

....

....

....

....

....

....

....

Date _____

God's Spirit - Your Instructor in Sharing Jesus' Light

The Holy Spirit inside you blesses those within your circle with Jesus' Love Light. But more amazing is that your Father-given, Son-given, Spirit-given Light will blaze even brighter as the Spirit teaches you in the Word how to share your Savior's Love Light.

And we all, with unveiled faces, beholding the glory of the Lord, are being transformed into the same image from one degree of glory to another. For this comes from the Lord who is the Spirit.

2 Corinthians 3:17b-18 esv

In your name, Jesus, I pray the Spirit will bless my mind and heart with his radiating wisdom on how to shine your Light on others. Amen.

[Jesus] But the Helper, the Holy Spirit, whom the Father will send in my name, he will teach you all things (enlighten you) and bring to your remembrance all that I have said.

John 14:26a esv

✦ ——— HEART THOUGHTS ——— ✦

Jesus blesses me with his Light when he ....

....

....

....

....

....

....

....

....

....

✦ ——— PRAYER OF GRATITUDE ——— ✦

Today, I'm thankful for ....

....

....

....

....

....

....

....

....

....

Date _____

DAY 94

No More Darkness, No More Night, Only Love in Jesus' Light

Ask God to cleanse your innermost
heart of darkness with his pure Light
who is his perfect Son. Be glad you cannot
hide sin. Rejoice that your Heavenly Father
wants to keep your heart pristine in the
Radiance of Jesus' Righteousness -
God's own divine brilliance.

Our secret sins - you (God) see them all.
PSALM 90:8B NLT

Thank you, Father, in Jesus' name, for showing
me my hidden motives and sins as you shine
your restorative Light into my heart. Thank you
for forgiving me and making me clean in your
presence based on my Savior's immutable
Righteousness shared with me. Amen.

*But if we freely admit our sins when his light
uncovers them, he will be faithful to forgive
us every time. God is just to forgive
our sins because of Christ.*
1 JOHN 1:9A NIV

⟶ HEART THOUGHTS ⟵

Jesus blesses me with his Light when he ....

....

....

....

....

....

....

....

....

....

⟶ PRAYER OF GRATITUDE ⟵

Today, I'm thankful for ....

....

....

....

....

....

....

....

....

Date _____

YOUR LIFE'S PURPOSE - PLEASING GOD WITHIN JESUS' SALVATION LIGHT

Be extravagant in thanking God for his Spirit gifts of Love, Light, and Life, just as he is extravagant in blessing you with salvation through Jesus' love gifts of grace and faith. Rejoice that your attitude of gratitude pleases your Heavenly Father who loved you before you ever loved him.

Oh, how sweet the light of day, and how wonderful to live in sunshine! Even if you live a long time, don't take a single day for granted.

ECCLESIASTES 11:7-8A MSG

Thank you, God, in Jesus' name for assuring me that my gratefulness for your Good News Gospel delights you. Amen.

The one who offers thanksgiving as his sacrifice glorifies me; to one who orders his way rightly I will show the salvation of God!

PSALM 50:23 ESV

DAY (95)

✦———————— **HEART THOUGHTS** ————————✦

Jesus blesses me with his Light when he ....

....

....

....

....

....

....

....

....

....

✦———————— **PRAYER OF GRATITUDE** ————————✦

Today, I'm thankful for ....

....

....

....

....

....

....

....

....

....

Date _____

CONQUERED - SATAN'S DARK LIES THAT LEAD TO DEATH! VICTORIOUS - JESUS' BRIGHT TRUTH THAT LEADS TO LIFE!

Jesus' Light blazes gloriously in Truth, while Satan's darkness fades to nothing in lies. God promises you in his Word that Jesus' Radiance leads to Life, even as Satan tries to hide the fact that his darkness leads to death.

The light shines in the darkness,
and the darkness can never extinguish it.

JOHN 1:5 NLT

Thank you, God, that Satan has no ultimate power as he spreads his malicious lie - evil is good, and good is evil - an upside-down, inside-out, shady philosophy doomed to be exposed by Jesus' Light of Truth. In the Savior's name, I pray my gratitude that his Truth is unchanging. Amen.

What sorrow for those who say evil is good,
and good is evil, dark is light, and light is dark,
bitter is sweet, and sweet is bitter.

ISAIAH 5:20 NLT

✦ ——— HEART THOUGHTS ——— ✦

Jesus blesses me with his Light when he ....

....

....

....

....

....

....

....

....

....

✦ ——— PRAYER OF GRATITUDE ——— ✦

Today, I'm thankful for ....

....

....

....

....

....

....

....

....

....

Date _____

JESUS' DIVINE LIGHT -
AWESOME, ASTOUNDING, AMAZING

If scientists can focus natural light from a laser sharply and accurately enough to cut through a diamond, think what God can do with his own uncreated Light that is his Shekhinah Light in Himself, in addition to his Word Light in Scripture and Word Light in Jesus.

The glory of the LORD shall endure forever.
PSALM 104:31B KJV

In your name, Jesus, thank you for your authenticity as God's Word Light. *The Word (Jesus) was God.* **JOHN 1:2 MSG**; *I (Jesus) am the Light of the World.* **JOHN 8:12B ESV**; *The words I have spoken to you — they are full of the Spirit and life.* **JOHN 6:63B NIV**. Amen.

His (God's) powerful Word is as sharp as a surgeon's scalpel, cutting though everything, whether doubt or defense, laying us open to listen and obey. Nothing and no one can resist God's Word. We can't get away from it, no matter what!
HEBREWS 4:12B-13 MSG

HEART THOUGHTS

Jesus blesses me with his Light when he ....

....

....

....

....

....

....

....

....

....

PRAYER OF GRATITUDE

Today, I'm thankful for ....

....

....

....

....

....

....

....

....

....

Date _____

PRAYER - YOUR DIVINE SPIRIT CONNECTION TO HOLY GOD IN THE RADIANCE OF JESUS

Jesus is your model for how prayer joins you
with the Light of God. Ask the Holy Spirit
to purify your prayers. Claim your Father's
promise in PSALM 112:4A NLT
Light shines in the darkness for the godly.

*Jesus took Peter, James, and John and climbed a high
mountain to pray. As he prayed, his face began to
glow until a blinding glory streamed from him.
A radiant glory illuminated his entire body.
His brightness became so intense it made his clothing
as blinding white as multiple flashes of lightning.*

LUKE 9:28B-29 TPT

Thank you, God, in Jesus' name, that
*the Holy Spirit passionately pleads before God for
us, his holy ones, in perfect harmony with God's
plan and our destiny.* ROMANS 8:27B TPT. Amen.

*Listen to my voice in the morning, LORD.
Each morning I bring my requests
to you and wait expectantly.*

PSALM 5:3 NLT

HEART THOUGHTS

Jesus blesses me with his Light when he ....

....

....

....

....

....

....

....

....

....

PRAYER OF GRATITUDE

Today, I'm thankful for ....

....

....

....

....

....

....

....

....

....

Date _____

JESUS' RADIANT DAYSPRING – SHARED WITH YOU IN HOLY LOVE

Jesus is God's Living Branch of Life and the Dayspring of His Light. Praise your Heavenly Father for fusing his own divine Life, Light, and Love into one meaning - Jesus Himself - God's Holy Word and Salvation Light given to you.

In that day the Branch (Jesus) of the Lord will be beautiful and glorious (Light-filled).
ISAIAH 4:2 NASB 1995

In your name, Jesus, thank you for shining your Light, Life, and Love on me. PRAISE YOU! Amen.

[Zacharias] For thou (John the Baptist) shalt go before the face of the Lord to prepare his (Jesus') way; to give knowledge of salvation to his people by the remission of their sins, through the tender mercy of our God; whereby the dayspring (Jesus) from on high hath visited us.
LUKE 1:76B-78 KJV

HEART THOUGHTS

Jesus blesses me with his Light when he ....

....

....

....

....

....

....

....

....

....

PRAYER OF GRATITUDE

Today, I'm thankful for ....

....

....

....

....

....

....

....

....

....

Date _____

JESUS' LIGHT - PRESENT IN HIM ON ARRIVAL, DEPARTURE, AND RETURN

Seek the Holy Spirit to keep your Spiritual lamp
trimmed and burning. Be joyfully prepared
to meet your Savior when he comes back.

[Jesus] *"Then the Kingdom of Heaven will be like ten
bridesmaids who took their lamps and went to meet the
bridegroom (Jesus). Then those who were ready went in
with him to the marriage feast, and the door was locked.
Later, when the other five bridesmaids returned, they
stood outside, calling, 'Lord! Lord! Open the door for us!'
But he called back, 'Believe me, I don't know you!'
So you too must keep watch! For you do not
know the day or hour of my return."*
MATTHEW 25:1; 10B-13 NLT

In your name, thank you, Savior, for the vital
message in **1 THESSALONIANS 5:19** ISV, *Do not put out the
Spirit's fire.* Lord Jesus, let me glow in You! Amen.

*Keep your lamps trimmed and burning, for this world
is almost done. Keep your lamps trimmed and
burning, for our race is almost run.*
GOSPEL SONG

DAY 100

✦ ——————— HEART THOUGHTS ———————— ✦

Jesus blesses me with his Light when he ....

....

....

....

....

....

....

....

....

....

✦ ——————— PRAYER OF GRATITUDE ———————— ✦

Today, I'm thankful for ....

....

....

....

....

....

....

....

....

Date _____

COMING SOON...

Look for Terry Ward Tucker's upcoming novel,
GOD HEARS YOU! Do you hear God?

Anne York spends her prayer time asking
God to grant endless personal requests...
until she discovers that her own life plans are
lame compared to her Heavenly Father's
thrilling plans. That is when Anne asks the
Holy Spirit to turn her self-focused chatter
before God into Father-focused, Jesus-focused,
Spirit-focused communion with her
Heavenly Father - *more listening, less talking -*
which transforms her life into its joyful best.

What about you?
Do you talk more or listen more
when communing with your Father?

GOD HEARS YOU! Do you hear God?

TERRY WARD TUCKER and her family are members of First Baptist Church in Charleston, SC. She holds a PhD in Reading Education. Her popular devotional book, *INSPIRE YOU DAILY DEVOTIONS,* was so well received by readers that Terry responded to their encouragement by writing *RADIANCE OF JESUS – One Hundred Devotions,* a new series for those who enjoy worshiping on the same page together, plus anyone else who wants to be blessed mightily by God's *Son*Light.

Terry's first novel, *Charleston's Elegant Sinners,* is set in the Lowcountry of South Carolina. Her second, *Moonlight and Mill Whistles,* received *ForeWord Magazine*'s Silver Book of the Year Award. Winston Groom, author of *Forrest Gump,* wrote, "Terry Ward Tucker tells a lovely and captivating story in *Moonlight and Mill Whistles.* Her writing is a joy to read." Terry's latest novel, *Moonbow Over Charleston,* is also set in the South. Pat Conroy wrote about *Moonbow,* "Terry Ward Tucker paints a moonbow upon Charleston's night sky and gifts us all with its loveliness. Thank you, Terry!"

Tucker served as screenplay co-writer for faith-based movie, *Only God Can,* produced by Inspire You Entertainment, and screenplay writer for *Hate Won't Win,* a new film in development based on the shooting massacre at Mother Emanuel Church in Charleston. Her upcoming novel - *GOD HEARS YOU! Do You Hear God?* - will launch in 2022.

Tucker came to Christ at age eight in a revival meeting at First Baptist Church in Lancaster, SC. She is thankful to be known as a born again Christian and hopes people all over the world will be as blessed by reading her daily devotions as she was by writing them.

MORE WORKS BY TERRY
(partial list)

INSPIRE YOU Daily Devotions (366)

Moonbow Over Charleston

GOD HEARS YOU! Do You Hear God?
2022 launch

Charleston Kisses

Moonlight & Mill Whistles

Charleston's Elegant Sinners
2023 pub date

Arlena Returns to Charleston
2023 pub date

ONLY GOD CAN
feature film, screenplay co-writer

Made in the USA
Columbia, SC
10 December 2021